CUSTOMERS
MEAN
BUSINESS

CUSTOMERS
MEAN
BUSINESS

Six Steps to Building
Relationships That Last

JAMES A. UNRUH
CHAIRMAN AND CEO
Unisys Corporation

⩕ Addison-Wesley Publishing Company, Inc.

Reading, Massachusetts   Menlo Park, California   New York
Don Mills, Ontario   Harlow, England   Amsterdam   Bonn
Sydney   Singapore   Tokyo   Madrid   San Juan
Paris   Seoul   Milan   Mexico City   Taipei

Material from Ch. 7 adapted from *On Becoming a Person: A Therapist's View of Psychotherapy* by Carl R. Rogers © 1961 by Carl R. Rogers. Courtesy of Houghton Mifflin Company.

Many of the designations used by manufacturers and sellers to distinguish their products are claimed as trademarks. Where those designations appear in this book and Addison-Wesley was aware of a trademark claim, the designations have been printed in initial capital letters.

Library of Congress Cataloging-in-Publication Data

Unruh, James A.
   Customers mean business : six steps to building relationships that last / James A. Unruh.
      p.   cm.
   Includes index.
   ISBN 0-201-59043-3
   1. Customer services—Management—Case studies.   2. Customer relations—Case studies.   3. Success in business—Case studies.
I. Title.
HF5415.5.U57   1996
658.8'12—dc20   96-15780
                                                          CIP

Jacket design by Suzanne Heiser
Text design by Diane Levy
Set in 11.5-point Sabon by G&S Typesetters, Austin, TX

1 2 3 4 5 6 7 8 9-MA-0099989796
First printing, August 1996

Addison-Wesley books are available at special discounts for bulk purchases by corporations, institutions, and other organizations. For more information, please contact the Corporate, Government, and Special Sales Department, Addison-Wesley Publishing Company, One Jacob Way, Reading, MA 01867, 1-800-238-9682.

Contents

CONTENTS

Preface

THE INFORMATION AGE is just half a century old, but its impact on business and government has already been extraordinary. From the moment in February 1946, when engineers at the University of Pennsylvania formally unveiled the ENIAC—the first large-scale programmable, general-purpose computer—to the present, when the Internet and the World Wide Web are transforming computing and telecommunications, information has become the defining resource, and its management one of the principal challenges, of our civilization.

The computer and communications systems that created the information-based economy have also created a buyer's market. Productivity has been increasing, and there is global overcapacity in almost every industry. As a consequence, price wars are rampant, and customers have the advantage in most transactions.

Customers are also better informed than they once were. Telephones, radios, televisions, faxes, and computers allow them to examine the attributes, prices, and services of the products available to them. Better-informed customers are more discerning customers. They want it all. High-quality, fully featured products at reasonable prices used to satisfy them. Now they're in a position to demand service—customized products and personal attention—and they're complaining that not enough companies are providing it.

Leading organizations—both commercial and governmental—are recognizing that to deliver on the customer service imperative, they must make use of the flood of information generated by their operations and their interactions with customers, as well as critical marketplace information, in fundamentally new ways. They must learn to think of information as an asset and use it to improve customer service and decision making. They must move from information processing—basically, what computing was about during its first half-century—to information management.

Examples abound of organizations that are managing information to serve their customers better. Hotel chains now remember their guests' accommodation preferences from stay to stay. Supermarkets record customers' selections at checkout counters and offer premiums and discounts based on past purchases. Kiosks in government offices help citizens receive benefits payments faster or make filing simple legal documents easier. Manufacturers allow customers to track the status of their orders or shipments on-line.

At Unisys, we developed a process, known as Customerize, designed to make businesses and government agencies more responsive to their customers. It requires focusing an entire organization—purpose, people, processes, and information—on serving customers and building lasting relationships. When an organization becomes truly customer-centric, the rewards will follow—greater profitability, increased revenues, loyal customers, and loyal employees.

As we developed the Customerize process, we wanted to know how other companies had established successful customer focus initiatives. To gain this understanding, we "went to school on the winners." We interviewed more than one hundred organizations that have been recognized worldwide for their dedication to their customers. We asked them how they direct every aspect of their organization—from establishing the vision to measuring the results—toward serving customers. We asked them about the benefits of this approach, as well as precisely how they did it. We encouraged the executives and managers we interviewed to speak freely and openly about their experiences. We weren't disappointed. They shared stories of what worked, what didn't, and what they planned to do differently to get even closer to their customers.

Now you can listen in on exactly what these companies told us about:

- How to disengage from unprofitable customers
- Why customer complaints are actually good
- How to select the right customers
- How to cultivate employees who truly want to serve customers
- How to appeal to what customers want in a service transaction—security, control, and self-esteem

The stories we heard were enlightening. We recognized common approaches among the winners, whether they were large or small, European or American, producers of tangible products like autos or intangible services like investment counseling. These best practices are action items; they represent the most innovative and effective things that world-class organizations are doing to retain customers, grow their businesses, and increase profitability.

The Customerize process brings the best practices together in one place and shows how they relate to each other. Once you've learned how the winners put it all together, you'll have the knowledge and tools to do it yourself.

Acknowledgments

THE REAL AUTHORS OF THIS BOOK are the organizations that participated in our research. Their experiences and advice are the heart of this work. Individually, but more often in teams, their key executives each spent at least two hours describing the details of the customer focus initiatives they had undertaken. They discussed how they got started, who was involved, where they made mistakes, and what secrets to success they uncovered along the way. We can't thank them enough for their time and frankness, and for the education they gave us on a critical topic. Our thanks also go to Stan Hunter and his team from Market Analytics, who conducted the interviews on our behalf. They did an excellent job identifying key concepts and innovative ideas.

About thirty of our research participants deserve special thanks. They agreed to attend intensive three-day workshops to discuss our initial findings with us, and to allow us to probe deeper into key issues. The spirit of sharing and camaraderie at the workshops was tremendous, due in part to the efforts of Bob Taraschi of TMP • Milestone, who facilitated the sessions for us. But even Bob was quick to admit that these sessions were unusual. The participants were eager to educate one another, sharing best practices about such things as customer listening and customer valuation techniques.

This book would not have been completed without the dedication of a key team of individuals at Unisys. One person in particular deserves special recognition: Jean Telkowski, who developed the initial summary of our research findings. It was her idea to build the report and book around the experiences of the research participants. This meant she had the arduous task of reviewing interview transcripts and workshop sessions to find the best practices presented here.

Howard Kearns deserves the credit for organizing and managing the research project. He was also first to recognize the value of our findings and to push to turn the research report into a book. From the research, Gary Payne developed the Customerize process, the six-stage process to help clients stay focused on customers, which is described in detail in this book. Dinyar Chavda made invaluable suggestions regarding the book's structure and content. He continues to bring tremendous insight to our ongoing research program. Dot Malson worked tirelessly to make sure that we actually published a book, and that we recognized its value within our community. Finally, Ellie McCarthy kindly introduced us to the world of book publishing and made sure that we had a coherent final product.

We'd also like to thank the many research participants who commented on earlier versions of this book. Their continuing insight and enlightenment are a joy for us. We hope they have benefited as much as we have from learning together.

Introduction

The customer is king!
—*John Wanamaker*
founder, John Wanamaker Stores

The customer is dictator!
—*Sir Richard Greensbury*
CEO, Marks & Spencer

The customer is God!
—*Michael Dell, CEO*
Dell Computer Corporation

IT'S AN UNDERSTATEMENT to say that the customer plays a vital role in today's economy. Governments, Fortune 500 companies, monopolies, and mom-and-pop stores all trumpet the importance of the customer. Unfortunately, not many customers are made to feel they are very important. In a pinch, they'd rather switch suppliers than fight. The few organizations that do understand and appeal to what customers value, however, are thriving, with growing, profitable businesses and, in the case of government agencies, satisfied taxpayers.

Organizations know that they must attract, develop, and retain profitable customers. The majority, however, do not know enough about how to do it. The legends of customer service that are often referenced in the literature—the Walt Disney Company, Nordstrom, and the Ritz-Carlton Hotel Company—are excellent role models. These companies were founded to serve customers, and they have set the standard for customer focus. Where organizations need more help is in understanding how to make the transition to becoming an externally focused, customer-centered organization.

This is their guidebook. It is based on extensive primary research with organizations that are recognized worldwide for their success in creating loyal customers. Among them are the legends of customer service, but the majority are companies that successfully made the tough transition to become pro-customer organizations. Their stories are inspiring.

The organizations that participated in extensive one-on-one in-person interviews and workshops for this book are head-quartered primarily in the United States, Canada, and Europe. Among them are Malcolm Baldrige National Quality Award winners and finalists, organizations certified by the International Standards Organization (ISO), CIO-100 award winners, companies in compliance with the Cadbury Code of Best Practices in the United Kingdom, and organizations recommended by trade consulates. The companies comprise a variety of industries: manufacturing, wholesale and retail distribution, finance, transportation, communications, utilities, and personal and business services.

The individuals who spoke with us include chief executive officers, presidents, and key executives of sales, marketing, manufacturing, quality, and customer service. The range of our interviewees reflects the fact that serving customers is the responsibility of many, if not all, functions within an organization. The people we spoke with willingly shared the lessons they learned in developing their customer focus initiatives. They talked about the problems they encountered and the changes they had to make in operations, goals, management practices, and employee attitudes and skills. They talked about everything that went into their customer focus initiatives—why they decided to focus on customers, how they listen to customers, how they enable employees to serve customers, how they develop long-term relationships with customers, and how they measure results and maintain momentum.

The stories of these research participants, presented anonymously *in their own words,* are the basis of this book. Their stories may be unique, but the participants created delighted, profitable customers in parallel ways. A major theme among them is that focusing on customers requires the dedication of the entire organization. Customer focus involves much more than developing a good customer service program and measuring customer satisfaction. In fact, there is a series of stages through which organizations can progress to develop their initiatives. Those stages are summarized as steps in the Customerize process, (see Figure Intro-1) and correspond to chapters in this book. At the end of each chapter, a section called Sound Advice summarizes the key steps in that stage.

The Customerize process is a holistic approach to organizational growth and profitability. It integrates and reconciles every aspect of an organization—purpose, people, processes, and information—to serve customers better. Nothing is left out of the process, and everything works together.

The stages or steps in the process are as follows:

Prerequisite: Obtaining Top Management Commitment.
The Customerize process can begin only if top management is committed to it. It is top management that enables an organization to focus on its customers. It leads the development of a statement of purpose centered on customers, communicates the vision constantly, and makes

sure that the organization's practices stay aligned with the vision. Most importantly, top management is a role model for the rest of the company in its own commitment to serving customers.

1. **Understanding Customers.** Once top management is committed, the organization must discover what customers *value*. What they value means more than what they think about product attributes and benefits. It means what they want, need, and expect from the seller. Another part of this stage is to examine how competitors are identifying customer values.

Figure Intro–1   **Stages of the Customerize Process**

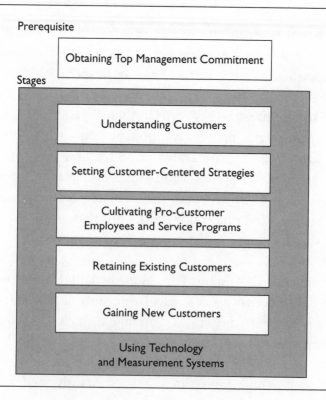

2. **Setting Customer-Centered Strategies.** An organization's strategy should be built around satisfying customer values—but not those of *every* customer or prospect. It should focus first on profitable customers, making adjustments as customer profitability changes over time. Second, it should select customers who fit its service capabilities—that is, to whom it can provide individualized service and who will remain loyal.

3. **Cultivating Pro-Customer Employees and Service Programs.** The best customer-centered strategy in the world is only as good as the employees' ability and desire to implement it. Organizations have to develop pro-customer employees—employees who proactively serve customers. This development takes place through staffing, communication, education, empowerment, and reward and recognition programs. Pro-customer employees are those who provide the services that customers are demanding. Today, customer service includes personalized offerings, extras, guarantees, individual attention, and abundant information about the organization and its products and services.

4. **Retaining Existing Customers.** Organizations that develop good relationships with their existing customers are more likely to keep them. The steps for building good customer relationships are very similar to the steps for building good personal relationships. They include accessibility, accountability, commitment, enhancement, and positive regard.

5. **Gaining New Customers.** Acquiring a new customer can cost five times more than retaining an existing one. Therefore, when organizations talk about gaining *new* customers, they often mean increasing share of wallet

from existing customers. Increasing share of wallet requires knowing customers so well, usually through
careful analysis of customer databases, that what they
will purchase and when can be predicted. This information is also used to selectively target new customers
who will be profitable, benefit from the organization's
services, and fit the profile of a loyal customer.

6. **Using Technology and Measurement Systems.** In each
stage of the Customerize process, information technology is used to enable and deliver customer service. Examples include database marketing, computer-integrated
telephony, and the most-talked-about service technology—the customer information system. Measurement
also takes place at each stage in the process. Top organizations understand the interrelationships among
financial performance, market position, product or service quality, employee satisfaction and retention, and
the all-important customer satisfaction and retention
measurements.

In today's information age, organizations do not have the luxury of time and investment to learn only from their own
experience. Global competitors are more numerous, bigger,
and faster; markets are converging; and customers are more
demanding. To survive, the intelligent organization must continually learn from customers, competitors, and successful
practitioners everywhere in the marketplace. This book gathers
the best practices of world-class customer-focused companies
and organizes them into six strategic steps that any organization can take to start or accelerate its own customer focus
initiative.

1

Getting Started

TOP MANAGEMENT COMMITMENT is necessary to enable an organization to focus more on its customers, as we will see in Chapter 2. But what convinces top management that they should make that commitment? This was the first question we asked our research participants. Figure 1–1 shows their answers. These companies realize the key role that retaining and attracting customers can play in improving competitive position. Other considerations—increasing profits, correcting service

Figure 1– 1   Reasons for Initiating Customer Focus

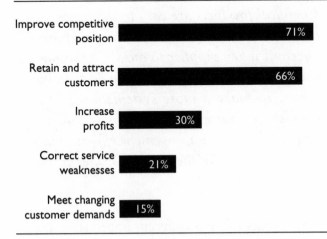

Note: multiple responses possible

weaknesses, and meeting changing customer demands—play only a secondary role in their decision-making.

IMPROVE COMPETITIVE POSITION

It used to be possible for an organization to establish and maintain a competitive advantage by offering superior products, prices, or quality. Although there will always be a few product or price leaders in every industry, top-quality, fully featured products at low prices are considered table stakes these days. Today, customers have shifted the battleground to providing superlative customer service—something that can't be duplicated easily.

A chemical company that participated in our research told us how it has added service to its traditional product offerings in its customer focus initiative:

> *We always thought of ourselves as a product company, but as we stepped into the 1990s, we recognized that service, as opposed to products, is something that is very difficult to duplicate. Chemical products are easy to duplicate; being responsive to customers is not. Our primary corporate objective is to become a key supplier to our key customers and to be competitive in the global market. To do that, our business units have to make a more systematic effort to survey our customers, measure customer satisfaction, and use those findings to drive the improvement efforts within our company. We intend to be the services leader in our industry.*

A bank we spoke to has taken a different approach—transforming traditional banking services into "fundamental" customer services:

The way banking is performed in our area is a cookie-cutter type of service. There is tremendous dominance by a few banks. We saw a market niche that told us to return to what we would call fundamental service, focused on the customer and not on a transaction. For example, instead of offering multiple types of checking accounts to confuse our customers, we offer one. Customers with higher balances receive interest, customers with below-minimum balances do not. Another example: Although it is more expensive for the bank to issue statements with a month-end cutoff, we do it because our customers prefer it.

Although superior service is hard to develop and maintain, it is becoming easier to find. In most industries, deregulation, globalization, and market convergence are creating even more competitors. In today's crowded marketplace, service either is or will become a key differentiator. The airlines that participated in our research had seen this change coming in the 1980s, with industry deregulation; the utilities were not far behind and could see it coming in the near future. According to one utility:

In the beginning of the 1980s, we were a monopoly. During the 1980s, we saw that we were going toward free markets, which would require changing the way we did business. Our CEO felt that before long it would be impossible for the telecommunications business to remain a monopoly. That meant that the development of a service quality program was necessary in order to be successful and competitive in the open market.

New competitors may come from outside traditional industry boundaries. In the United States, for example, banks are watching investment firms, who are watching insurance companies, who in turn are keeping their eyes on the banks. Competitors may also come from outside traditional geographic boundaries, as they did for this American auto manufacturer:

Historically, a Japanese luxury car was unthinkable. But in the 1990s, Japanese luxury cars are among the best. The key to their success wasn't only quality—it was service, the special treatment the dealers provide to their customers. For example, top management is required to call two customers a week in order to get a better understanding of their needs. Customer comments are often fed into new product design. There were seventeen hundred changes made to one of their 1995 models—each one was customer-driven.

No matter what part of the world they come from, competitors will invariably find new ways to serve customers. This manufacturer had to change its strategic focus to emphasize service in addition to product quality in order to compete:

The competition was providing a whole new playing field. They were identifying new customer needs for individual treatment and long-term partnerships. They forced us to go beyond product quality. To survive, we had to go beyond what we had done. We had to invest in customer focus, relationship building, and organizational alignment.

Generally, it's much easier to ignore customers than to pay attention to them. Therefore, our American research participants in particular often developed a customer focus initiative in response to their concerns about survival. These participants noted that many challenges to their survival were coming at them, from both inside and outside. These challenges included the disappearance of competitive advantages, market deregulation, consolidation of distribution channels, advertising failures, customer defections, employee departures, deterioration of business processes, slow growth, and declining profits.

For example, the advent of fewer, larger distributors for its products forced this candy manufacturer to focus more closely on satisfying customer needs in order to survive:

> *For years we had a fairly homogeneous mass of customers that bought pretty much the same product lines, same quantities, and seasonal business was only a minor part of the overall industry. The market environment changed within about a ten-year period. Channels of distribution were consolidating, and the distributors were trying to find unique ways to distinguish their offerings. The timing, frequency, and types of products they purchased changed dramatically. This compelled us to start looking at customers in very different ways—based on their own unique characteristics. I guess you could really say it's part of a survival strategy. But it's also part of a strategy to keep pace with a very dynamic environment. It forced us to really segment our customers by classes of trade, by size, by geography, and by the characteristics of their buying organizations (centralized or decentralized).*

An airline adopted customer service to survive the crisis brought on by industry deregulation:

> *The company was making money quarter after quarter, and then that just ceased. Prices were dropping precipitously; competition was fierce; and customer loyalties were becoming very, very thin. Fewer customers were accounting for a higher percentage of revenues. The CEO's*

strategy for survival *was differentiation from the competition: being dramatically better in a single discipline—customer service.*

RETAIN AND ATTRACT CUSTOMERS

If American companies ranked their competitive position, or even their survival, as their number-one reason for focusing on customers, our non-U.S. research participants ranked customer retention and attraction as their number-one reason. While the American companies seemed to have a more defensive posture when it came to customer focus, non-U.S. companies were much more offensive.

For example, this European manufacturer recognized the connection between better service and its goal of gaining higher market share:

> *Our goal was to increase market share, and to do that we had to have better service. Customer satisfaction levels and renewals were still very high, but it became clear that we really had to break out of that mold to increase share. Business as usual was simply not good enough; our level of service had to go up a notch.*

Emphasizing the customer is not revolutionary. An ancient Chinese proverb states: "Customers are the precious things; goods are only grass." This philosophy guided successful businesses until the Industrial Revolution. One of the research participants gave his impression of how this worked:

> *Before the Industrial Revolution, the proprietor of the general store met and knew every one of his customers. He knew the kinds of goods each one bought, and he adjusted*

his inventory to fit their changing needs. His business was built on his relationships with his customers and what he knew and remembered about them. His memory allowed him to solve their problems individually and thereby to sell more products to each.

The Industrial Revolution and the advent of mass-produced goods changed the way business was conducted. Manufacturers focused on building brand equity to distinguish their products from the thousands of others on the marketplace. They relied on mass media to cost-effectively promote their products to millions of potential consumers and to build demand. Individual marketing and customer service were generally overlooked, according to this car manufacturer:

Back in the good old days, employees actually said, "We'd have a great operation if those customers wouldn't keep coming in with their requests." The customer was kind of the enemy. What the company wanted was to have a sweetly running factory or have service occur without a hitch. Customers were problems because they kept asking for things that were different from what the company wanted to give them. The attitude used to be: "We'll figure out what we can make, and you'd better want to buy it." We make, you take. We speak, you listen.

Today, advances in technology have made it both possible and practical to reestablish the types of customer relationships that existed prior to the Industrial Revolution. Companies now have the capability to gather, analyze, and use information in order to better know and serve their customers individually. They are relearning the ancient traditions of respect and friendship for customers, but this time they are able to apply them to many more customers in a fast-paced marketplace. The business philosophy of this steel manufacturer echoes the marketing approach used by the proprietor of a general store in the days before the Industrial Revolution:

Today, what's good for the customer is good for the company. It's a complete chain. It starts with manufacturing and goes right up to the customer's shop. It involves going beyond traditional marketing techniques and entering into a relationship with your customers—giving them a sense of satisfaction with the purchase decision they have made; letting them know that you recognize and value their business; showing them you understand their needs and will respond to them; making them feel special, needed, wanted—not just as consumers or prospects but as individuals. Our efforts should be viewed as the process of managing customer relationships over an extended period of time. This approach gives us everything—high-quality products, reliable processes, loyal customers.

INCREASE PROFITS

Putting the focus on customers leads to increased profits. Our non-U.S. research participants were twice as likely as U.S. participants to cite financial rewards, particularly increased profitability, as resulting from improved customer service. One of them said:

We put together a proposal that showed if we did certain things, we would be able to cut our costs considerably, about $75 to 80 million dollars a year. At the same time, we would have an order-of-magnitude better service. Profitability was our primary objective, and our continued

success in an increasingly competitive market would de-
pend on our position as the best or leading customer ser-
vice provider.

How does customer focus increase profits? Companies that
know *what* and *when* to sell to existing customers can sell more
often at a price premium. Satisfied existing customers also refer
new customers, who cost less to recruit and are more likely to
buy. And when a company focuses on the things that matter to
customers, its costs decline as unnecessary and inefficient operations are stripped away. At a time when many companies have
tried and failed to downsize, rightsize, or reengineer themselves
to increased growth and profitability, customer retention may
be the better way.

Our research participants have experienced the following
kinds of financial returns from their customer focus initiatives:

- Increased sales, particularly good volume increases from
  top customers who identify the company as a preferred
  vendor. As companies got to know their customers better, cross-sales of new products also increased.

- Referral customers, who cost nothing to acquire and
  usually arrive predisposed to buy. One hardware chain
  estimated that as much as 50 percent of its sales is the
  result of referrals.

- The ability to charge higher prices—usually between
  5 and 10 percent. Customers perceive the increased
  value of the company's precisely targeted products and
  services.

- Lower costs. It's much more expensive to find a new customer than to sell more to an existing customer.

- Increased revenue from long-term customers. Car dealers estimate that a loyal owner is worth from $300,000 to $400,000 over a lifetime.

- Increased profit from long-term customers. Typically, profit per customer increases as companies understand better what their loyal customers want, and customers get what they expect from their suppliers and have fewer problems.

Some of our research participants measure the benefits of focusing on customers by calculating the costs of customer *dissatisfaction*. An auto manufacturer explains this point to his dealers:

Our customer satisfaction survey has two questions: Would you buy again from this dealer? Would you recommend this dealer to a friend? If the customer checks "definitely not" or "probably not," then the dealer has lost future sales—repeat and referral. Typically, the gross profit on one sale is a thousand dollars. So for every unhappy customer, the dealer loses a thousand dollars from repeat business and many more thousands from lost referrals. Unless, of course, the dealer can change the customer's attitude and right what's gone wrong.

One research participant who was about to enter a deregulated environment put the case quite simply:

If there is no customer, there is no money. If there is no money, there is no company.

CORRECT SERVICE WEAKNESSES

Complacency, arrogance, or ignorance can cause companies to lose sight of why they are in business—to serve customers. Surprisingly, it is sometimes the most successful companies that lose touch with their customers, and they find this out only when growth starts to slow:

> *For fifteen years, we were ahead of the competition, and we got a little complacent. We grew at 25–30 percent a year. Then, all of a sudden, that 25–30 percent growth started to show up as 22 percent one year, and maybe 18 percent several years later, then 15 percent. We realized that some changes had taken place. We weren't as close to our markets. We decided that we had to find out what was going on, and fix it.*

Arrogance can also cause service operations to deteriorate. Sometimes customer focus initiatives start as a way to correct service weaknesses. That was the case for this research participant:

> *Customer service used to be a skirmish between striving to keep a lid on service and support costs, and customers who wanted as much free support as they could get. The service level was right when customers were "sullen but not rebellious." Unfortunately, this attitude toward service caused customers to leave us. This forced us to take a closer look at our customer service operations and to make changes.*

Now many organizations are making customer service a top priority. Sometimes, as this computer manufacturer points out, someone from outside the traditional company culture is needed to highlight the importance of service:

The conventional wisdom around the company was that our customers thought we were difficult to do business with. There were horror stories—a guy placed an order, and all these terrible things happened to it. This happened because the company thought its job was to make complex, expensive products. Then we hired someone with a consumer marketing background. That person started doing market surveys, finding out what was important to our customers. We found out that the things that were of a high-tech nature weren't what was most important to our customers. The most important factor was service.

MEET CHANGING CUSTOMER DEMANDS

Today, customers are more knowledgeable and demanding than they were even a decade ago. They make better-informed purchase decisions and spend their dollars wisely. Because they assume that quality will be built into every product they purchase, they have very little patience for shoddy workmanship. With more choices available, they have *no* patience for unsubstantiated high prices.

Lacking meaningful ways to distinguish among good products, customers have decided to do business based on how they are treated. "Is it easy to do business with this company?" they ask themselves. "Are the company's employees working mainly for the company or for me? Are the company's products easy to use?" Customers are expecting—and demanding—not merely satisfactory but superior service. One research participant described this change in customer values:

A few years ago, people would buy the lowest-priced product. Today, customers look at the total cost of buying a product as compared with just the sale price. If your product is at a slight premium, but everything you ship is on time and top quality, the total cost of doing business with you might be less than with a company that sells a cheaper product.

And customers are no longer shy about demanding what they want. An angry customer caused one company to start focusing on service and quality:

A prominent customer gave our company president the new message: "If your company doesn't get involved in satisfying customers, we're going to stop buying your junk products. We have other choices now." That encounter went further than any other message to commit the company to service and quality.

Companies that fail to listen to their customers often find they have fewer customers to listen to, as this company discovered:

When we asked customers why they were leaving, they gave three reasons: service, service, service. Not providing adequate service became a very expensive strategy. For each customer that left, it took five or six new customers to make up for the lost revenue.

Customers often define service as personal attention; they want to be understood, treated as individuals, and pampered. Serving customers means developing customer relationships—relationships that are based on long-term commitment and trust. Today, the dynamics and scope of customer relationships are changing.

Customer relationships start at the first meeting between buyer and seller. Sellers use this opportunity to educate potential buyers about their products, leaving it to the buyer, the more powerful partner in the relationship, to make the sale. All types of companies now utilize this marketing approach. A manufacturer of pharmaceutical products calls this a "tell, don't sell" approach:

> *People want to be sold to, but not by the foot-in-the-door approach. They want to be advised and helped. If not, they will push back. Selling is a different game today.*

An investment counseling firm echoed this approach:

> *Our customers said, "Don't give me your pitch—just give me the facts, and let me decide what to do with them." We have millions of customers. We can't possibly know them well enough to give them great advice. What we can do is provide lots of educational help so they can make their own decisions.*

Customer relationships have also become broader in scope. Companies are encouraging their employees to develop relationships with customers outside the business setting. In an informal atmosphere, it's often easier to get to know customers as individuals. A bank has its employees use their environmental clean-up days to get closer to customers:

> *When we conduct our environmental clean-up days, we make sure that our customers are invited to come along. Each year we work alongside our customers to clean up*

the local area. It's a positive event; we both take pride in what we're doing. This kind of atmosphere makes it easier to get to know our customers as people, not just corporate accounts or wealthy investors.

A car manufacturer relies upon customer enthusiasm for using its products to bring it closer to its customers:

Our dealers have a special relationship with their customers. They take the time to organize weekend road rallies for them. We tour different parts of the country together. This is a great opportunity for the dealers to get to know customers better, to show that they care, and to start to build a stronger relationship. The customers get to ask questions about the company and its products; any individual problems can be addressed separately one-on-one. The customers also get to meet and share experiences with other owners who share the same enthusiasm for the company's products.

TAKING THE PLUNGE

The decision to focus on customers and pursue a relationship strategy is a daring step, and often the future is unknown. There is no up-front way of knowing how much effort, time, or money will be required. Organizations learn by doing, but very few regret making the effort:

I remember in the early years of the service initiative questioning whether we should make the investment. We struggled. Can we afford all the elements of the initiative, such as employee training and development and new measurement systems? Looking back, I can only wonder, how could we have afforded not to? It's a no-brainer. But at the time, we were nervous. It was expensive, but the payback was quicker than we expected.

A management directive for better service, such as the one issued by the chairman of this company, can easily raise concerns, but ultimately there were no qualms:

One day the chairman decided that customers' questions about money should be answered in no more than twenty-four hours, and he gave us three months to figure out how to do it. We weren't sure this was the right thing. Did we have to go that far? Could we do it? In hindsight, I can see he was right.

Our research participants have another piece of advice for companies just starting out. Customer focus is not an organizational program that has a defined beginning and end; rather, it's an ongoing process. Progress will be slow, but the results are well worth the time and effort:

You have to be committed. Go for it! Once you get started, don't stop. Customer focus is going to cost you money. It's an ongoing process. The measuring bar is raised constantly by the marketplace. It's not something that's going to be a key for us this year, and next year it's kind of on the back burner. If you have that attitude, you're not going to win.

SOUND ADVICE

Even if an organization isn't focused on its customers, its competitors are. And the customers know where to find those competitors.

In the buyer-seller relationship, the balance of power has shifted to the buyer. Buyers are demanding personalized service and partnerships with sellers—and they're getting them. Companies that provide what their customers demand are recouping financial rewards. If your organization hasn't already made the customer the focus, now's the time to start. This is the age of the customer.

Customer focus is not a one-time-only program. It requires a permanent ongoing commitment of *all* organizational resources.

2
Obtaining Top Management Commitment

THE STARTING POINT for any customer focus initiative is obtaining top management commitment. Unless senior executives are committed in both word and deed, employees and customers will dismiss the initiative as another "program *du jour.*" Our research participants cited top management commitment as the number-one requirement for a successful customer focus initiative. In fact, they consider it a prerequisite.

One company explained the importance of having a pro-customer CEO by describing what happened when that CEO was replaced by one less committed to customers:

> *Our CEO retired. In his place we had a CEO who said our customer focus initiative was a "good idea. Keep me posted." This is not what you would call sponsorship. Slowly, our efforts started to unravel. The lesson we learned is that senior management is the leadership of the organization and must be behind the initiative.*

MANAGEMENT NEEDS CONVINCING

Some companies, like Nordstrom, the Walt Disney Company, and the H.J. Heinz Company were founded by individuals who were already devoted to serving customers. Others happened upon the strategy by accident. A telephone company that participated in our research described how its CEO convinced his neighbor to choose his company's telephone after promising that it would be installed in four hours instead of the normal two days. The neighbor was so grateful that the CEO decided to make this level of service available to all customers. Soon this company had made serving customers a top priority.

According to another research participant, market forces can play a role in convincing management of the need for change:

> *There was a fundamental shift in the marketplace after the stock market crash of October 1987. The vast majority of the investing public who relied on their full-service brokers to make decisions for them realized that their brokers weren't always right. As a result, the public began to say things like, "I'm not going to let anyone make all the decisions with my money, and I'm going to take responsibility for my own investments." Instantly, a whole new world opened up for us, where the focus has been to educate and provide assistance so our customers can competently take responsibility for their own investments.*

More often than not, though, the decision to focus on customers is a consciously planned event. According to our research participants, a company's key sales and marketing executives—those who are closest to its customers—are usually the ones to convince CEOs to pay more attention to customers. The reason is that these marketing executives see every day that focusing on customers can improve the bottom line.

But top management needs proof before it can make the commitment. Generally, customer focus sounds like the right thing to do, but it can also sound complicated and expensive. Showing management the benefits of customer focus that other companies have achieved can help them make the right decision, according to our participants. Figure 2–1 shows the areas that improved because of customer focus initiatives for firms in our research. These benefits support the reasons they originally decided to focus on their customers (Figure 1–1).

Comparing Figures 1–1 and 2–1 shows some good news: The financial rewards of customer focus were actually greater than the organizations expected them to be at the outset. This is definitely the most convincing argument for why management should adopt a customer focus initiative. The companies also reported that their competitive positions improved, and they recorded higher levels of customer satisfaction and retention. One research participant described their success:

Our operating profit doubled. Inventory went down a third. That's over a billion dollars in savings. Customer satisfaction increased 20 points. That's an average—the actual increases ranged from 8 points to 46 points. Market share in most businesses improved dramatically.

Figure 2–1   **Areas That Improved Because of Customer Focus Initiative**

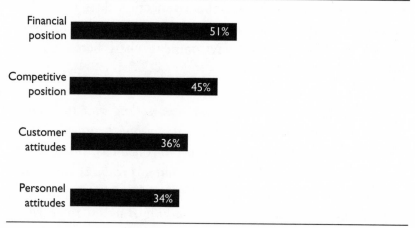

Note: multiple responses possible

Another participant used quantitative *and* qualitative measures of success:

Stemming lost customers has increased our revenue. It has increased sales. It has increased profits. It is a measurable, demonstrable change. It has increased the number of clients we can use as references and the number of clients that would recommend doing business with us. It has increased our ability to deal with our customers and suppliers as partners. It's achieved its original intent, which is far better customer service: it's teaching us what customers really want, what really matters to them. We're getting closer to that than we ever have before.

Figure 2–1 shows another unexpected benefit from customer focus: improved attitudes on the part of employees. Focusing on serving customers gave employees a better understanding of their roles and enhanced their desire to perform them well. Consequently, employee satisfaction and retention increased.

Improved employee attitudes and morale, in turn, benefit customers. When employee satisfaction increases, so does customer satisfaction. However, this connection does not tell the whole story. For one research participant, customer focus has created an improved work environment where better business decisions are made:

Salespeople are spending more time selling and planning with customers and less time justifying problems and issues. Among other things, their improved customer focus and understanding have led to better products and advertising. The image of the company has also improved, enhancing the stock price and making it easier to recruit top-quality people.

For another research participant, customer focus has made for a more pleasant working environment, where employees have more fun doing their jobs and hence do better jobs:

The company's focus on service quality has actually made the company a better, fun place to work. It's eliminated barriers between organizations, frustration over inability to coordinate resources on behalf of the customer, and confusion over organizational responsibilities. By empowering and enabling employees, decision making has been streamlined. Responsibility and accountability for decisions that impact customers have been given to the people who interact with customers. This has resulted in faster decisions, happier customers, and a more motivated, creative, and informed workforce.

Time and again, the research participants remarked that their customer focus initiatives have increased employee accountability and teaming. Said one:

Employees work together much, much, much better now. The company's service quality initiative not only simplified business processes, but it simplified the organizational structure by reducing layers of management and giving greater authority lower down in the organization. In the past, there were little fiefdoms operating very separately. Now there is one global organization that is integrated very well.

START AT THE TOP, BUT DON'T FORGET THE REST

While top management commitment to a customer focus initiative is key, commitment must also come from other levels within the organization. Employees can't be commanded to serve customers; they have to *want* to serve them. Two companies found that they could foster employee commitment by involving their employees in the process of defining customer-centered strategies. Both companies used employee surveys to gather opinions for the development and execution of their strategies:

There was, within the organization, a tendency to think that senior management creates something and then sells it to everybody. To change that impression, the company surveyed its sales associates to determine its customer strategy. Over three-quarters of employees felt the company was not giving enough emphasis to customer service. The survey further identified what employees felt should be done: things like better training of new sales associates and improved customer delivery procedures. The approach was really one of finding out what the people who are close to the customers say needs to be done, and then aligning the organization to accomplish that.

This company obtained very valuable employee input from a survey about the applicability of its new advertising slogan:

The marketing department launched a slogan: "You Can Count on Me." The employees told us that if the customers are going to count on us, then we'd better improve our ability to be counted on. A survey of sales associates revealed five areas, such as sales floor procedures and inventory position, which they felt needed to be improved to reach the standard implied by the slogan.

COMMUNICATE THE VISION

World-class service providers have vision statements that are focused externally—on customers and competitors. They talk about providing "100 percent customer satisfaction, 100 percent of the time." One company had a goal to be the "best service provider in its industry," then changed its goal to becoming the "best in service provision period." Another company stressed the linkage between customer satisfaction and empowered employees in its mission statement:

Our mission is to develop one knowledgeable and empowered employee, one service contact, and one satisfied customer.

Once a company agrees upon the vision, employees need to know that top management is committed to realizing it. In these ever more turbulent times, employees want the meaning of an enterprise to be compelling. Moreover, for the vision to take hold, management must constantly communicate it. Our research participants reported that employees overwhelmingly prefer to hear the vision directly from management rather than read about it in memos or company publications. Sometimes this requires executives to get out of the head office and meet one-on-one with the employee population:

The chairman of the board went "on the road" with the company's vision statement. He visited employees all over the world, asking them for their personal buy-in. He stood on the back of a truck in an airport hangar talking to two thousand employees at a time.

Customers also need to hear the company vision. One-on-one meetings with customers can convey it to them, but some executives prefer to stay in more frequent contact with their major customers by picking up the telephone:

Every other week senior executives at this company make phone calls to major customers to find out how things are going. They bring them up-to-date on any new company initiatives, then they ask questions: "Are there any major problems you're having with our company? Would you recommend our company in the future?" It's a very personal call. If the customer wanted something improved, the executive would note the details of the request. If possible, action would be taken to meet the customer's requirement. The result of the action was monitored by the senior staff so that they were aware of progress made before the next phone call to the customer.

Reinforcement of the vision at every opportunity—in meetings, letters, and broadcasts—is important. This bank's chairman is constantly checking with his employees to see if the vision is being upheld:

At every conference or meeting the chairman is always asking: "What does this do for our customers? How does this benefit our customers? Do we have all the services we can provide for them? Do they have money with us and money with one of our competitors? How do we get that back?" Always those questions! The culture the chairman has created is almost frenetic: Make sure that every customer has every need satisfied!

BE A ROLE MODEL

Top management must act as a role model and show by their actions that they are listening and responding to the concerns of customers and employees alike. Customers and employees believe what they see. Often, an unusual show of commitment makes the longest-lasting impression. The chairman of an airline regularly checks on operations at four o'clock in the morning:

> *The new chairman of the airline would arrive at terminals at four in the morning to talk with check-in personnel. He also checked the cleanliness under the airline seats. Now middle-level managers do the same thing. Years later, the chairman still stops by at four A.M. to check on things.*

The president of a bank checks with customers on Tuesday nights:

> *Every Tuesday night, the bank president goes to a different branch to meet with fifteen to twenty customers. The customers present their suggestions for improved service, and they're not always polite. Nevertheless, the president listens, and the bank has introduced numerous services and product offerings in response to these suggestions.*

Smart executives also take employees' comments seriously and respond appropriately. For example, one company's employees suggested that their leaders weren't visible enough. In fact, some said that they didn't even know *who* top management was. Senior management responded by instituting regular "town meetings" to communicate to staff where the company has been and where it is going. The employees could ask questions, comment on programs, and also offer suggestions and new ideas through special 800 numbers and e-mail. Members of the leadership team personally responded to all calls and letters. Then the leadership team members went one step further: They made employee responsiveness part of their personal development plans. Executives take these plans very seriously because their compensation depends on achieving the goals set forth in them.

For one organization, these employee-focused actions had an unforeseen benefit: They created greater understanding and respect among levels of the organization that did not normally work together. This new sense of community helped strengthen the caring and organizational ownership among all employees:

Every executive at this firm spends three hours a month fielding calls from customers. This requires them to be up-to-date on the company's products and procedures. The executives have also developed a great deal of respect for the people who sit alongside them on the phones. A program geared toward communicating with customers has actually improved communication, dedication, and morale among all employees.

LEAD BY ENABLING EMPLOYEES

Top management must not only establish the organization's customer-focused vision and act as a role model; they must lead and motivate all employees to realize that vision. In a fast-paced, uncertain world, the need for strong leadership has never been greater. It is no longer enough for executives merely to preside over their organizations; they must lead and guide them. This leadership, however, must be more than visionary and more than the old-fashioned command type.

A leader may have a quite impressive ability to command respect and deference, give orders, and ensure that those orders are carried out. But in today's complex organizations human energy is mobilized by empowering people with ideas and information, not by telling them what to do. This is known as enabling leadership. Enabling leadership is absolutely necessary in an environment where *all* employees are expected to act on behalf of customers. Enabling leadership is based on company values:

Leadership is not about giving orders; it's about honoring feelings. Most particularly, it's about honoring the feelings of your subordinates, creating an organization that fulfills its highest potential because it is guided by values and not *by the personal considerations of the leader.*

Sound values and enabling leadership can be inspiring:

We have too much management in our organizations today and not enough leadership. We must leave behind the traditional preoccupation with the organizational structure and its processes and move toward a much more diversified thinking process that focuses on the creation of value, mobilizes collective intelligence, and projects an inspiring vision of the organization. Only in this way can we bring every resource to bear to serve customers.

Leaders must also be team builders. Building a team means putting the right people in the right places, teaching them to work together for each other and for the customer, capitalizing on their individual strengths and resources, and continually developing them both as a team and as individual leaders. One executive calls this indirect leadership:

> *Only by demonstrating depth and strength of character is an individual ready to assume the responsibility of leading others who are themselves leading a team. This is the work of indirect leadership. It requires an intimate knowledge of the individual employee's capabilities and of how best to bring people together as teams—teams, that is, that are best suited to serving customers.*

Finally, leaders keep the organization focused on what it values—its customers. One executive found that focusing on values creates common bonds that engender trust and a willingness to work together:

> *Use the organization's value system to forge the bonds that tie the organization together. Common values create trust, and it is trust that holds a team together. This approach takes constant care and attention.*

Although he didn't say so, focusing on external values also keeps an organization from focusing too much on internal politics.

SOUND ADVICE

Don't start a customer focus initiative without top management commitment. Employees and customers won't take the effort seriously. It will end before it's had a chance to begin.

Top management commitment means:

- establishing, preferably with the involvement of all employees, the organization's vision to serve its customers

- communicating the vision constantly to all employees and customers

- acting out the vision by regularly serving customers

- leading the organization by enabling all employees to adopt the organization's vision in their day-to-day activities

3

Understanding Customers

ONCE TOP MANAGEMENT is committed to building an organization that serves customers, the next stage of the Customerize process is to learn what customers need and value. Customer needs and values should influence every aspect of the organization: strategy, employee staffing and performance, product and service development, sales and marketing programs, operational procedures, and information and measurement systems.

Understanding customers is crucial to the success of any customer focus initiative. It is also very complex; it involves learning not only what customers currently value but what new values are being created by competitors. The techniques for uncovering values have also become more numerous and time-consuming to implement and analyze. So it's not surprising that our research participants said they made the most mistakes in this area. Too often they thought they knew what their customers wanted without asking them. Or they asked their customers questions that management thought were important. Or they were not truly listening to customers or observing their behavior:

> *In the beginning, we asked ourselves what customers wanted. It took some time for us to recognize that we should be asking customers directly what they wanted: "We want to hear from you. We need to hear from you."*

LISTEN!

The first step in understanding customers is to listen to them. A company needs to hear what its customers are saying about its people, products, services, and vision. To find out what customers really think, some companies let the customers themselves develop the questions they want to be asked. This way a company can learn what is truly bothering or delighting them and hence what is truly important to them. No matter how it's done, however, listening to customers must be an ongoing process, and the results must be communicated and put into use throughout the organization.

> *Initially, a company focuses on its customers by listening to them. You can't take that for granted. You have to define ways that work for the company. This may include conducting small focus groups with customers, or listening to incoming customer calls. Listening has to be ongoing and disciplined, and the information has to be played back into the business and used.*

Organizations need many different kinds of information about their customers. Obviously, they want to know what customers think about them, their products, and their competitors, but they also need to know about the personal lives of their customers. This information helps them develop meaningful products and services. One direct-mail company has developed a wealth of details about its customers. It captures more than a thousand pieces of data on each customer, ranging from behavioral characteristics (such as categories of clothing purchased and preferred price points) to personal details (lifestyle preferences, family members, and key purchase events like birthdays) and financial status (payment profile and credit score).

Our research participants collect the following kinds of information to get to know their customers better:

- Product/service history
- Competitive experiences
- Satisfaction rating
- Complaints
- Suggestions
- Preferences
- Family characteristics
- Life events
- Hobbies
- Pet peeves

Companies often collect this information during the course of customer phone calls. One company encouraged its employees to spend *more* time on the phone with customers, to establish a personal rapport and gather the relevant customer details:

> *We encourage customer service representatives to establish personal links with customers. We capture information about birthdays, new jobs, new cars—anything that the representative may want to inquire about in future calls. The average customer call is five to six minutes. Customers are willing to discuss all kinds of things—compliments, competitive references, suggestions, and complaints. We definitely collect many more good ideas than complaints.*

Another research participant feels so strongly about developing complete customer profiles that it has a major calling program under way to gather historical details about its key customers:

We've been calling our major customers to understand the extent, the history, of our relationship with them. We're asking them about how many of our products they have installed and about prior contact such as service calls or complaints. We want to know as much as we can about them so we can provide the best service.

Even organizations with millions of customers are trying to learn more about their customers as individuals. In this way they hope to discover what customers truly value in their products and services, and in their relationships with the organization. The companies also hope that getting to know customers better will show their customers that they care about them and can be trusted to serve them well. Companies want to develop personal relationships with their customers. As described in Chapter 7, personalizing the buyer-seller relationship helps to develop loyal customers—and increased sales.

This new approach requires that frontline employees learn how to care for customers: to find out who they are, what they need, and how best to serve them. Although this transition may be difficult for some organizations, the good news is that most customers enjoy getting the attention, and most employees appreciate their new role. This company is encouraging its employees to take customer care to an even higher level—to be "passionate" about customers:

We are teaching associates to talk to customers in a different way, a more friendly way, and teaching them to listen better. We're trying to get them to stop thinking of customers as one type or another and to start thinking of them as individuals. This is all about engendering some passion for customers.

What customers value goes beyond the obvious product attributes and benefits to include customer needs. Needs are often implicit, unarticulated, and unstated. They include things like freedom, security, and peace of mind. In the hierarchy of customer values, shown in Figure 3–1, product attributes are at the bottom, benefits are on the next level, and implicit needs are at the top. Companies that appeal to needs will achieve far superior performance to companies that address only product attributes or benefits. A car manufacturer applies the hierarchy of customer values to the purchase process:

The typical conversation with a prospective buyer starts at the attribute level, discussing such things as airbags, miles per gallon, comfortable seats, and well-placed console. Why does the customer want these things? Usually because of benefits such as driving ease, safety, and reliability. Underlying the benefits are usually one or a few

Figure 3–1   The Hierarchy of Customer Values

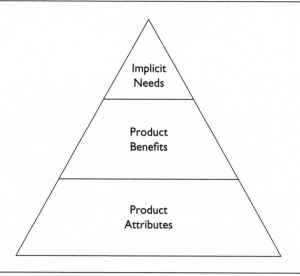

ultimate needs, such as peace of mind. Our best sales-people know how to keep asking customers questions until they uncover needs. If a company can determine what customers truly need, it can achieve much greater results because all efforts can be targeted at fulfilling the desired need.

LISTEN TO *ALL* CUSTOMERS

Organizations need to listen to *all* their customers: satisfied, dissatisfied, neutral, and prospective. As one company executive said, "Talking to satisfied customers is like talking to myself"—unless, of course, the satisfied customer is also using a competitor's product or service. This comparison can be very enlightening:

We continually ask customers what the competition is doing that is delighting them. What kinds of product improvements have they been making? Do they have new service standards? How do they listen to their customers? We don't want to be blindsided by a service imperative from the competition.

Dissatisfied or departed customers can also provide tremendous insight into customer values that aren't or weren't satisfied. Listening to these customers can be more difficult because the values and ideas they mention are often ones that companies have never considered. Where warranted, a company should make changes based on what it has heard:

A closed account study of high-balance accounts revealed that certificates of deposit (CDs) were a big product that we were losing to mutual funds. Not surprisingly, these consumers were looking for the highest rates and the low-est fees. What we really learned when we dug a little deeper was that the majority of people wanted flexibility and liquidity at a competitive rate. We used that information to propose a no-penalty, liquid version of a CD.

This company takes the learning process a step further, involving customers in solving their problems:

We make a point of talking to people who no longer fly our airline to find out why and what it would take to win them back. We also talk to dissatisfied customers. For example, if someone said on a recent flight that they didn't like the meal in economy, we ask why. Then we bring them in to test a new product.

Finally, it is important for organizations to listen to people who have yet to try their products and services. These individuals can test whether the company's customer values still make sense. Sometimes, as this company found, prospective customers can suggest new values that can be addressed and new markets that can be targeted:

Regularly we survey households in the areas surrounding our grocery stores. We try to understand why people are or are not shopping with us. In one urban market, a key customer value was convenience. People were busy and wanted to spend less time grocery shopping. In fact, one customer suggested: "Why can't I send you my grocery list and have you shop for me?" This got us thinking about a "shop by fax" service. We tested the concept and found that there was a market of sufficient size for this service in our urban areas. Now we are reaching a new type of customer with this service, and they have remained very loyal.

LISTEN TO EMPLOYEES

Listening to what employees say customers are telling them is just as important as listening to customers themselves. It serves two purposes. One is to obtain input from those closest to customers. The second is to show respect for employees' opinions, thereby increasing their motivation to serve customers well. This company finds it useful to ask employees what customers think about its products and services:

> *We ask employees what they think of the services the company provides to its customers. Are they the right services? What are the customers saying? We also ask employees to judge services that are under development. What do they think? What will the customers think?*

Sometimes management is surprised by what employees tell them. This company has turned its surprise into action, requiring that management spend more time listening to customers in the future:

> *When we decided to become a service leader, we asked our employees what they thought customers expected of the company. Four qualities led the list. Two were expected— the care and concern demonstrated by employees and the ability of frontline personnel to solve problems. But the other two were eye-openers. Contrary to what management had imagined, employees felt customers were also concerned with how spontaneous and flexible employees were in applying company policies and with their ability*

to recover from mistakes by making things right for the customer.

Some of our research participants feel so strongly about the importance of listening to customers that they require *all* employees to listen, even those who don't normally come into contact with customers. It may involve something as simple as listening to customer calls or meeting with customers occasionally, or something more complex like undertaking customer research. One company stressed the importance of conducting market research at the local level, since such groups can understand and act upon what they have heard sooner:

> *We encourage each geographic area to conduct client research. This way each local area can better understand its clients' needs and expectations and develop marketing programs accordingly. Each local area can also respond much faster to client issues.*

Employees are also encouraged to listen to those people at the customer site with whom they don't normally meet. This company put its sales representatives in closer touch with its customers' executives. The discussions resulted in better service and happier customers:

> *We want to get our people back in the clients' locations, even our corporate staff. Get out of the building and spend time with customers. Listening is a contact sport! Our customer-care plans require a monthly meeting with customers, where we get all the department heads together to review their issues. Being face-to-face with all the users made a big difference. We were able to uncover true customer concerns, as opposed to what we thought were*

customer concerns. Solving the right problems resulted in better product utilization and higher levels of customer satisfaction. We also made a point of listening to executives. We used to deal primarily with operational employees who had objectives that were different from the executives'. So we were getting trapped. Now we pay attention to both the decision and implementation levels. Our efforts actually helped open up communication within companies.

LISTENING TECHNIQUES

As shown in Figure 3–2, our research participants listen to customers in a number of ways, ranging from formal surveys to informal meetings.

Most companies already have traditional listening systems—satisfaction surveys and customer research—in place. Almost half of our participants have also recognized the importance of

Figure 3–2   Customer Listening Techniques

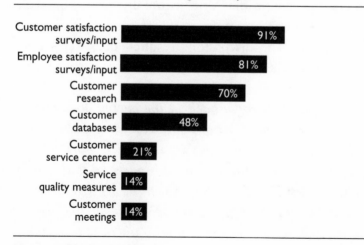

Customer satisfaction surveys/input   91%
Employee satisfaction surveys/input   81%
Customer research   70%
Customer databases   48%
Customer service centers   21%
Service quality measures   14%
Customer meetings   14%

Note: multiple responses possible

customer databases. Best practices regarding these systems and their use as measurement tools are discussed in Chapter 9.

The major trend among our research participants is to improve their customer listening systems, even the broad-based ones, so that they can gather and analyze *individual* customer data on a *continual* basis. Consumers' needs change frequently, and customer listening systems have to be capable of reporting the details.

Customer service centers are where employees deal frequently with many different types of customers. There, too, prospective customers are mined for detailed information. Today, companies advertise their service centers, to make it easy for their customers or prospects to communicate with them. They list their 800 phone numbers and fax numbers on all their products. Some open their e-mail systems, encouraging customers to contact them to get information on product use, to obtain service, or to make a complaint. The Internet is an increasingly popular means of two-way communication.

> *We keep product and pricing information on the Web. We also include an on-line purchase order. Now companies can easily and quickly place their orders with us. To make the connection more personal, we include pictures and profiles of employees who have contact with customers. This way customers can see and get to know the person they're talking to over the phone, or the person who may stop by for a visit.*

The requests for information or service made to a customer service center, which typically make up 60 percent of contacts, provide tremendous insight into what customers want and need. One company has its customer service representatives identify the top ten customer issues each week. Then the customer service staff meet regularly with product managers and design staff to discuss those issues. Marketing and engineering use the weekly top-ten list to enhance current products or develop new ones.

A very small percentage of contacts are customer complaints. Our research participants caution that complaints, contrary to popular belief, are incredibly valuable. Complaints indicate where things have gone wrong—where customer values are not being recognized or addressed. One research participant feels so strongly about complaints that it periodically advertises in newspapers for customers to "please, please, please complain." They do this to overcome customers' natural reticence to complain. Most companies' surveys show that only 3 to 5 percent of dissatisfied customers complain, and that percentage is even lower in some cultures.

Like customer values, though, a company must analyze the complaints if it is to understand what is truly upsetting its customers. A bank research participant cited an example:

> *A customer calls to complain about his current account, but it's usually not really his current account that's causing him to complain. It's not even his statement that's causing him to complain. It's not even the entry about the penalty charge on the statement. It's the fact that the statement was late. He likes it on the first of the month, and it didn't arrive until the fifth.*

Focus groups are another means to obtain detailed information about customer values. One company abandoned the traditional blind focus group approach in favor of meeting with its customers for dinner. It found that these meetings fit better with its desire to get to know its customers as individuals.

At first, we had managers sit behind a one-way mirror and listen to a facilitator discuss issues with customers. Although this technique was useful, it didn't really enable the managers to probe customers and "connect" with them. Now the managers take customers to dinner. Usually two executives sit at a table with six to eight customers, and they listen to what the customers say; and the customers are quick to describe what they like and don't like. Most of them use competitors' products too, so we also get comparisons.

Customer teaming is another one-on-one listening approach. Customer teams are groups of customers and employees that regularly spend time together to get to know each other. The employees use the teams to identify what's important to customers, based on how they use the company's products and services. The teams can be composed solely of executives, or they can be cross-functional. They can meet at the customer's site or on the company's premises. They can discuss anything from long-range plans to operational glitches. Although the team members may change over time, the teams remain in existence so that the company and its customers can continually learn from each other.

For one of our research participants, the teaming process started at the top of the organization, then was improved by including all levels:

It starts with top-to-top meetings. Our top executives meet with a customer's senior level executives to discuss long-range strategy, business plans, and whether customer needs are being met. It's like having external directors on your own board of directors, except they are your customers.

Management was hearing what customers wanted, but the operators weren't so sure. So we had teams of operators visit customers so they could understand customers' expectations firsthand. They'd meet with their counterpart in the customer's plant, recognize a problem, develop a solution, and see how it was implemented. They appreciated what downtime meant for a customer and how they had to catch up. Management supported the process. If operators needed funding for the solution, it was provided. With the addition of the operator teams, customer collaboration took place top-to-bottom and across functions.

Another company has found value in allowing its customers to spend time at its facilities. Together, customers and employees can review whether the company is conducting business in a way that serves customers best.

We brought clients into our factories and support organization. They spent a week or two learning how the company operates. There was some risk involved, but overall it was a positive experience. They understand better how we produce and service our products. They were even able to make suggestions about how we could improve operations to better fit their needs. For example, we've made dramatic improvements in how we package our products for shipment to make them easier to assemble.

All these customer listening methods are geared toward continual customer listening. Listening once a year is simply not enough anymore. One airline we interviewed plans to take continual interaction to a new level, capturing customer feedback immediately:

We conduct customer satisfaction surveys in-flight and at the end of the flight. We even video customers at the end of the flight and use the videos to train frontline staff as well as senior and middle managers. We are considering placing interactive video screens in the seatbacks. This way customers can provide instantaneous feedback about all aspects of the service: departure/arrival, aircraft cleanliness, food quality, and so on.

ANALYZE THE INPUT

After asking, listening, and teaming with customers, an organization must analyze what customers have said. Too often the analysis stage is overlooked. Either the data are scattered throughout the organization, or no one has clear responsibility for analyzing it, or both. Sometimes technology can provide a solution. Advances in parallel computer processing and data warehousing can bring together customer data that are spread among different computer systems and "mine" it for patterns in what customers are buying, why they're buying it, and what they'll buy next. For example, supermarket chains regularly analyze reams of demographic data, historical buying patterns, and sales trends to determine just where to open their next stores and how to stock them.

One of our research participants uses a customer input management system to analyze customer data and educate employees:

We have a number of listening systems in place, but they're not well orchestrated. We have a customer complaint system, but it's used primarily to respond to complaints—not for analysis about prevention and improvement. We have market research data, but it's not being used across the entire business. We have a transaction-based customer survey, but the results aren't related to any other customer information. So we're in the process of developing a customer input management system. This will serve two purposes. One, it will consolidate the input from all the listening systems so the input can be analyzed. Two, it will make the results available on-line to all employees so they know what our customers are saying and can look at complete individual customer profiles. These changes are about getting back to fundamentals and paying attention to how to better use information that is available already.

Once information is brought together and analyzed, the organization must make sense of it and do something about it. One organization recommended cross-functional customer review boards as a way to alert the rest of the company to its customers' needs and to improve performance. The review board members typically come from sales, marketing, manufacturing, engineering, and customer service.

Once a month, we convene a customer review board. We review the reasons why customers are leaving, comments from customer contact surveys, comments about customers from employees, response center findings, and focus group results. All these comments are brought together in one place, and follow-up actions are determined.

As we will see, the information that an organization gleans from its customers, particularly concerning what they value, is crucial in determining its strategy, employee development, service programs, marketing tactics, information systems, and performance measurements.

SOUND ADVICE

Understanding what customers value is the foundation of a successful customer focus initiative. Unfortunately, it's also the area that often gets the least attention, usually because organizations think they already know what their customers want.

Understanding customers requires much more than conducting an annual customer satisfaction survey. It requires listening very closely to who customers are and what they like and dislike. This calls for continual, one-on-one listening whenever possible. Organizations also need to listen to potential customers and to employees to uncover values that customers themselves may not recognize they have. Finally, everything that's been heard must be continually analyzed to create a complete and accurate picture of the customer. This view should be reflected in an organization's strategy, processes, people, and systems.

4

Setting Customer-Centered Strategies

LISTENING TO CUSTOMERS and studying the output provide organizations with a base to set strategies for aligning themselves with customer values. Strategies should address questions such as, "Who are my customers?" "What customers do I want?" and "What business do I want to be in?"

Figure 4–1 shows the various inputs used by our research participants to develop a customer-centered strategy. Smart companies get help from both inside and outside.

Figure 4– 1 **Strategy Input**

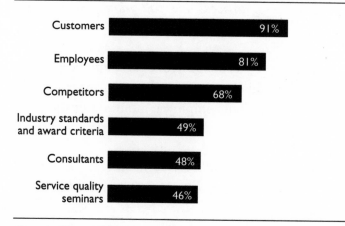

Customers	91%
Employees	81%
Competitors	68%
Industry standards and award criteria	49%
Consultants	48%
Service quality seminars	46%

Note: multiple responses possible

GATHERING THE NECESSARY INGREDIENTS

One way to make sure that a company's strategy is absolutely customer-focused is to involve customers and employees in its creation. Doing so will help the strategy meet customer objectives, and employees will be able to implement it. One company achieves this synthesis by inviting customers, employees, and members of its board of directors to review its plan:

> *Every year we invite customers to headquarters to discuss their expectations for the next five years. In addition to customers, the meeting includes approximately a hundred employees, suppliers, and members of the board of directors. We start the meeting by parading our five-year plan, including such things as service, quality, and on-time delivery standards, in front of mother, God, and country. It's rich to have customers and suppliers in the room at the same time listening to the vision. Then there's a feedback mechanism for them to either applaud or go boo, hiss! The outcome of the meeting becomes part of the long-range strategic plan. In addition, the plan is communicated to every employee—a process we call management by planning.*

Another company gets feedback from its employees about when its priorities should be changed, using its measurement systems. It also actively solicits employee input about the competition's strategies.

> *Our employees participate actively in raising the bar for customer satisfaction and performance. They establish the areas in which they will be measured that translate into quality performance: things like, "How quickly do you respond to a call?" or "How effective is your dealing with*

the customer?" Real-time feedback is provided regularly to employees. They analyze the data to determine when additional training is needed, or when processes may need to be reworked or improved, or when our goals need to be changed. Employees are also encouraged to keep an eye on the competition. These data are used for planning purposes. A monthly report, compiled in part from employee feedback, is circulated to all employees to encourage them to be alert to what's going on in the industry and to make necessary adjustments in their daily activities to stay ahead of the competition.

In addition to customer and employee input, companies examine what their competitors or other best-in-class companies are doing. Competitive analysis can give insight into competitors' strategies, capabilities, strengths and weaknesses, culture, and personality. It provides a thorough understanding of what competitors are trying to accomplish, how they will do it, how likely they are to be successful, and how they will respond to changes in the marketplace and *their own* competitors' moves.

Some companies choose to study their competitors firsthand by having their employees use competitors' products:

We have three or four people who do nothing but travel on our competitors' airplanes. They provide analyzed and anecdotal feedback. They tape-record the entire flight. They time it. They record what the competition does—the nice touches—what they don't do well, and their customers' complaints.

Benchmarking is the next step after competitive analysis. It helps companies rigorously measure their performance against "best-in-class" companies within a given functional or process area. Benchmarking measures not only *how much* an organization can improve but also *how* it can improve by identifying best practices and key success drivers. Benchmarking is about improving competitive positioning and using best practices to stimulate radical innovation rather than just seeking minor incremental improvements in performance. Because of its external focus, benchmarking seems to aid most in establishing realistic measures of productivity and customer satisfaction, and in strategies that have an outward perspective.

There are three types of benchmarking. Organizations can benchmark against the top competitors in their industry, against industry competitors who are best at a particular practice, and against the world-class company that is recognized as *the* best at a particular practice regardless of industry. One of our research participants described its benchmarking activities:

> *We're constantly tearing down competitors' products to see what they're doing. We've also done some benchmarking against our better competitors. We have a few good competitors that make us run faster and harder. But frankly, in terms of new service initiatives, we've had to look outside our industry to find what could be called "best of breed." We've milked our own industry. Now we're looking at Federal Express Corporation and Walt Disney Company.*

According to the research participants, benchmarking is not an easy process; nor is it an inexpensive one. It's important for an organization to focus its efforts where they will do the most good. First, it should determine which processes are the most integral to the creation of profits. Those are the processes to benchmark, simply because improving them will have the most direct effect on the bottom line. The second key element is to make sure that *all* employees are involved in the benchmarking process.

Instead of the CEO or president going out to find best practices, cross-functional teams of employees go out and learn from the top companies. Ultimately, it's the team that will have to implement the practice and make it cascade throughout the organization. For example, when we heard about just-in-time manufacturing, we sent a team of people to see it in action. They learned about it, brought it back, and implemented it.

One company that participated in our research, a hospital, turned its benchmarking exercise into a collaborative relationship. Its managers asked the hotel they were benchmarking to serve as their teacher to help implement best practices. The hospital and the hotel also found novel ways to increase each other's business. For example, they developed a program that makes it easy for people to come to the hospital for a complete health checkup and then spend the evening at the hotel. A hospital administrator described the benefits of the program for both organizations:

Both institutions rely on frontline employees to satisfy their clients. The hotel's theory about its employees is to do unto others as you would have them do unto you. There's a natural tie between the two institutions in terms of how we regard our employees and our customers. But the hotel's been focused on customers longer than we have. So we had a lot to learn in that area. We've been focused on giving excellent patient care without the added piece that these patients and visitors are also our customers. The

hotel staff found, as is often the case in a teaching environ-
ment, that they gained a greater awareness of themselves.
Seeing how they could help the hospital brought about a
sense of purpose and rededication to the hotel's philoso-
phy. When people show others how to do something, they
reexamine their own processes.

In addition to benchmarking, the many service quality standards, seminars, and award criteria spawned by the focus on
quality that started in the 1980s can also help in developing a
strategy. Our research participants did caution, however, that
the standards should be applied selectively; only those most relevant to a company's customers should be used.

We examined a lot of industry standards such as Baldrige
[Malcolm Baldrige National Quality Award] and ISO [In-
ternational Standards Organization] to determine aspects
of our service initiative. We tried to have an open mind
about these guidelines to determine if they would have
value for our business. If there was value, we adopted the
idea. One of the mistakes that can be made is to accept the
guidelines blindly and focus on a set of requirements that
were developed by somebody that doesn't know your cus-
tomers. This can be a very easy way to lose contact with
what's important to customers.

This company believes that broader guidelines are better, but
the caveat about applicability is still relevant:

The more broadly the guidelines represent what is happen-
ing and what is needed, the more valuable they are. But
they can't be taken as gospel. They have to be applied to
specific situations. You have to understand what they

mean to you and your customers, and then decide which ones work, fit, and are important, and then use them.

STRATEGY BECOMES CULTURE

To be successful, a customer-centered strategy has to become part of an organization's culture. It cannot be *merely written on a piece of paper.* It has to become second nature to all employees, who will then improve upon it by learning from each other, their customers, competitors, and the general business environment.

For one research participant, implementing the company's service strategy has affected every aspect of the organization:

> *The approach to serving customers is systemic. There isn't an easy way to do it. Everything is interconnected and builds. In order to delight customers, you need smooth manufacturing processes, which means you need an accurate warehouse, which in turn relies on a good manufacturing requirements planning system and good suppliers. You can't accomplish one without the other. Every process has to come up a notch. It sounds simple, but it's very complex.*

Organizations, like people, learn in a fairly simple way, as illustrated on the left-hand side of Figure 4–2. They start with information, decide on a strategy, develop a plan, and take action. The hope is that action will result in an advantage, although sometimes we also learn from our failures. The hard part is to learn from outside the organization. This involves much more than identifying the hottest business trend. It requires identifying what customers need, what competitors are doing and planning to do, and how to take advantage of future trends in the marketplace. This kind of continuous learning is what creates competitive advantage.

Organizations warn against underestimating the amount of time and effort required to make serving customers a part of an organization's culture. Our American research participants, in particular, complained about the slow rate of organizational change.

The commitment to the customer has to be part of your organization. It has to be incorporated into how you do things. And it takes time because of the need for some change in behavior and culture. People have to start putting customers first, not their own departments. I don't think you can change the culture of an organization overnight. Programs need to evolve, people need to learn and develop, and organizations need to learn and develop. It takes some time to get everybody on board and going in the right direction. Learn the techniques, learn from your mistakes, and learn from others.

Figure 4–2   The Learning Loops of an Intelligent Corporation

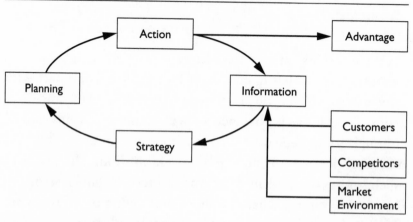

In fact because of the time involved, organizations also need to *plan* to refresh the initiative to keep it from getting stale.

A company can't stop its commitment to its customers. It can't start a campaign, do it, see that it works, and then move on to something else. Six months later the problems will be back again. It has to be an ongoing responsibility. Part of that responsibility involves actively planning to reenergize, revitalize, and relaunch the program. You need to learn continuously from others—customers, competitors, and other companies. Don't leave it too long. Stick with it to win—it's a bumpy ride!

Employee teaming seems to play an important role in helping organizations implement a customer-centered strategy. The teams can break down organizational boundaries and solve problems faster, and they can speed up the process of building a new culture.

We ran into a lot of turf/political battles in making the transition from a product-driven to a customer-driven company. To facilitate this process we created an umbrella organization that had very strong leadership and involvement from top management. The umbrella group has three committees, which meet monthly. The Corporate Committee sets policy direction for all activities. The Management Committee decides which programs should be developed. The Customer Satisfaction Committee makes sure that all departments, and not just Customer Relations, take responsibility for customer satisfaction. Every operational department serves on the committee and is assigned to subcommittees by problem area. The subcommittees are not limited to specific boundaries such as sales or marketing. They can cross over and work with each other. That was one of the key objectives of establishing the committee—to break down departmental boundaries.

TARGET THE PROFITABLE

Discussions about a customer-centered strategy usually lead at some point to a reanalysis of a company's customer base. Once a company has examined who its customers are, it starts to think about who it wants its customers to be. One research participant has found that it is easier to implement a strategy that has clearly defined target customer groups.

We operated for a number of years without an understanding of our target customers. Without that, it was very hard to develop a clear strategy on how to approach customers. Many parts of the organization were doing their best work, but this never created a sustainable service initiative or a corporate identity that could be marketed.

Most companies have a typical bell-shaped curve of customers: a few unprofitable or very profitable customers, and the majority barely or moderately profitable. The goal is to increase the number of profitable customers.

Although customer profitability is harder to determine than product or departmental profitability, it can be done. One company, an office supply store, realized that companies with fewer than fifty employees were its most profitable customers. Larger companies were less profitable because they had greater service requirements, which were better suited to the large mail-order supply houses. Other companies that have determined customer profitability include airlines that target Frequent Flyers, and banks that target wealthy customers with more than one product requirement.

For their profitable customers, companies are willing to do more, not only because of the customers' profitability but also because the customers will likely make valuable referrals. Some companies make a special point of focusing on their referral sources, treating them as a target group. For example, the mortgage department of a bank works hard to satisfy realtors who they expect will refer mortgage buyers. Similarly, travel agents are courted by cruise lines, resorts, and tour companies.

The search for profitable customers has led some companies to create customer segments, based on their customers' decision-making processes. Companies like this pharmaceutical manufacturer want to make sure they pay attention to the people who control the purse strings.

> *In the hospital business, there are a million different layers to the purchase decision, and changes in the industry, like health care reform, are adding to the complexity. We used to target the pharmacist or nurse who delivers the product and the patient who uses it. But the health care professional is not necessarily the decision-maker anymore. More and more that responsibility is taken by the hospital administrator. Pricing is also being set now at the hospital group level through regional buying groups. Even the hospital's decision-making authority is being usurped by the regional health care system.*

A department store, upon analyzing the buying processes of its customers, found an unexpected set of decision-makers:

> *Through market research we discovered that women make a lot more of the purchases in our store than we realized.*

Even in departments like hardware, men's wear, and paint—traditional male departments—women make up a significant percentage of decision-makers.

A customer's profitability should also be assessed over that customer's lifetime. The sources of profit include not only the original sales volume but also the potential for increased sales, cross-sales of related products, indirect revenue from referrals, and lower costs associated with serving familiar customers. The value of a customer relationship is determined primarily by three factors: volume, margin, and duration. The optimal value proposition requires a careful balance among all three.

We go the extra mile for customers that are very profitable for us. We want to make sure that they are satisfied with us, stay with us, and refer people who look just like them. Profitability is something we monitor throughout the customer relationship. While we are willing to devote the resources necessary to make these customers happy, we watch that we don't overspend.

Profitability changes over a customer's lifetime; therefore, companies need to know just how profitable a customer is, or will become, in order to decide which customers they want to acquire, develop, and retain. A bank looked at the changing profitability of one large target group:

This is a state that has a tremendous number of students. We really devote a ton of energy to the student market. Other banks, right or wrong, have walked away from this segment, saying that they can't make money. We do make money, and we also know that many of these students will be our customers in later years. We try to be smart about where we allocate our resources, and we look constantly to see where we are making or will make money.

SEGMENTATION STRATEGIES

Traditionally, segmentation strategies have categorized customers according to demographic characteristics or class of trade. More and more, though, companies are conducting needs-based segmentation. Such segmentation addresses customers' demands for service and personal attention. In some cases, segments are being "humanized," becoming almost personality types. Many different types of companies, like this chemical products manufacturer, utilize these strategies:

> *We developed needs-based segments based on the decision-making profiles of the individuals who purchase our products. We studied what was important to them and how they buy our products. The segments we developed include, for example, one-stop shoppers, no frills, advisory relationships, and service intensive. We trained all our sales representatives in proper probing techniques to identify each segment. But it's not round peg, round hole—it acts as a guide. Then, based on profiling, we determine what products and services we can provide to those customers to meet their relevant needs.*

A very different company, a bank, also conducted needs-based segmentation:

> *We surveyed our customers about their attitudes toward finance and identified three types:*

Anxious: What happens if I let go of my ATM card? Will I ever get it back?

Traditionalist: I have an account with this bank because my parents had an account with this bank.

Connoisseurs: What's new? What's innovative?

Customer needs change over time, and organizations that are astute enough to serve customers during critical periods in their lives create very loyal customers. A communications company provides an example:

Over people's lifetimes there are certain critical life events, like the birth of a child, when their communication needs are greatest. Why not lend mobile phones to people during these times? If these customers can be satisfied during these critical periods, they'll be customers for life.

Some organizations specifically target customers with whom they can develop lifelong partnerships. These customers act as sounding boards for new ideas and strategies. They are selected based on more than volume and margin calculations. They typically feel strongly about the value offered by the company, they buy at regular prices, and they refer other customers. They are also willing to discuss their future requirements and participate in a partnership. One research participant described the benefits of this approach:

The more these special customers teach us about their preferences and needs, and the better we become at providing what they want, the harder it will be for a competitor to entice them away. Even if a competitor were to provide the same offerings, the customer would have to spend an inordinate amount of time teaching the company what we already know.

Care needs to be taken in introducing segmentation programs. Those that single out customers for special attention should be implemented in a way that does not offend remaining customers. One bank described how *not* to implement a segmentation strategy:

Through an analysis of our account holders, we defined a segment of priority service customers and a whole set of marketing programs to support them. We launched the program with a banner at our main office that read, "If You're a Priority Customer, You Don't Have to Stand in Line." This slogan didn't go over well with our other customers: "What, I'm not a priority customer?" There was absolute chaos at the bank that morning, and a very short-lived segmentation strategy. In hindsight, we realized that the segmentation strategy was right—it was the implementation strategy that was wrong.

Although segmentation can help organizations understand their customers and develop appropriate products and marketing programs, the ideal segmentation program is invisible to the customer. People like, rather demand, to be treated as individuals. For customers, the only relevant segmentation strategy is the "segment of one."

We have so many customers, and for years, we've tried to put customers into categories. Every business does that. Then we try to shape and model our service programs by type of customer. We found that this approach is not really the answer. The answer is for each technician on-site to take care of the customer in whatever particular way they want to be taken care of. It isn't that we should be handling five different kinds of service delivery—we should be trained and able to deliver individual service.

This individualized approach can be realized even by companies that have very large customer populations:

Even though we have 28 million customers, we're trying to treat our prime customers as individuals. We've gone through several phases of redefining and learning about this approach. We focused first on major business customers under competitive threat. Now we're trying to understand how to segment residential customers. There are all sorts of segments of that market which revolve around customers' activities, relationships, and life events. Then customers change. Our strategy requires constant attention.

Top companies often combine all these segmentation strategies to create a new, more powerful, cost-effective approach to targeting customers. Called multidimensional segmentation, it combines attitudinal segmentation with demographic and behavioral research to identify target groups, where they are, and how to reach them. A bank used this approach to define a target group for its new gold credit card:

The starting point became the consumer segments already on hand, i.e., creditworthy people who are moderate-to-heavy users of credit cards, and who have overdraft credit lines. Next, we needed to know about the customers' attitudes toward using credit cards. Through quantitative surveys, it was possible to flesh out attitudes, discovering whether customers perceive the credit card as a substitute for carrying cash or as a symbol of financial success and prestige. Now we knew about these customers as people. Both behavior—through a review of credit card use and payment records—and demographics, through zip code overlays, enabled us to target and find this group rather easily. Now we had information-rich, actionable segments.

TEST THE STRATEGY

Once companies know who their customers are and what they value, they can decide on their strategy. Some companies change their strategies significantly as a result. A bank changed its focus from addressing savers to investors:

We always thought of our customers as savers. As a bank, our strategy was to safeguard our customers' money. Then we looked at what our customers were doing with their money, and at the phenomenal success of companies like Merrill Lynch, and we realized that our customers were not savers but investors. Today the business of banking is about safeguarding and growing our customers' financial assets.

The research participants recommend testing the strategy in a small part of the organization before implementing it fully. This approach will confirm the adequacy of the strategy while saving time and money in the long run.

We met with a consulting firm to discuss how we should start our service initiative. The consultant recommended "going single file. Take one affiliate, implement your initiative there, and show success. Then bring in the other affiliates to kick the tires and really understand what's going on. Use that affiliate as a model, and then roll it out." But we were in a hurry to make up for lost time, and we rolled out the initiative worldwide. In hindsight, we should have followed the consultant's advice; it would have saved time and increased acceptance.

This company chose to test its strategy among a small group of customers:

We rely heavily on one small group of accounts that uses everything we offer. These demo accounts serve as case studies of how services can be integrated to provide an efficient and productive relationship for both of us.

Another company tested its strategy by implementing it in one product line at a time:

Instead of changing every product, we selected one product line at a time, based on priorities. This strategy gave us the freedom to make little mistakes along the way without jeopardizing the entire operation.

SOUND ADVICE

A good strategy takes what an organization has learned about its customers and turns it into a workable plan of action. A strategy defines how a company will create value for its customers.

Strategies cannot be developed in isolation. They require input from customers, employees, and industry experts, then must be checked against the competition. Implementation of the strategy requires employees to realize it through their daily responsibilities.

One of the most important elements of a company's strategy is to identify the customers it wants to serve. Otherwise, it may try to be all things to all people. It should first select profitable customers, then categorize them according to their service needs so that they can be treated as individuals. Company resources are then aligned to satisfy the selected customers' requirements.

5

Cultivating Pro-Customer Employees

THE BEST CUSTOMER-CENTERED STRATEGY in the world is only as good as the employees' ability and desire to implement it. Employees are key players; they manage the moments of truth with customers. They are also responsible for developing long-term customer relationships. In fact, some companies, like this airline, claim that their employees are so important that they are the company's "products."

> *In a service business like airlines, it is the employee who's going to deliver the product. If they're not sold on the product and they're not rewarded for what they do, then you have a very tough time creating a better product, because they are, in fact, the product. The seats on the airplane are the same, the meals are the same, all of that is the same as the competition. There's not a lot to do that's much different. So employee attitude is the only difference. That's where you really have to make your mark.*

Most organizations, even those outside the service businesses (that is, businesses such as hotels and repair shops), are beginning to realize the connection between dedicated and happy employees and happy customers. A company that was, until recently, a monopoly made this linkage the centerpiece of its efforts to become a customer-focused organization in a competitive marketplace:

We came to a realization that if we were going to please our shareholders, the best way to do that was to delight our customers. If we delighted our customers, they'd keep buying more and more from us, and that would please our shareholders. The best way to delight our customers was to dazzle our employees, the people who work here. The direct linkage between these three groups provided the foundation for the steps we took to build a customer-centered organization.

This chapter examines how world-class companies involve, develop, enable, and motivate employees to serve customers. The next chapter looks at how these companies design and implement customer service programs that support employees' efforts to serve customers.

PEOPLE WHO LIKE PEOPLE

The steps taken to develop employees are much the same as those taken to develop customers. The first step is to hire the right employees.

Organizations want employees who have a propensity to serve—that is, people who genuinely like people. Some organizations rely on personality questionnaires or psychological profiles to find them. One company uses a long-term hiring approach to find employees best suited for customer contact positions:

We used to put applicants through about two hundred hours of testing, interviews, and site visits with other representatives before hiring them. We recently changed that policy. Now, whoever wants to become a representative must work for the company for three years, in any capac-

ity, before even being considered. Then they go through an extensive, six-month-long training program, followed by an even more intensive internship program. We think this will give us an employee who has a sense of our philosophy and a kind of built-in loyalty to the company. We'll know considerably more about them—their work histories, capabilities, and talents—before we enter them in the selection process. In addition, the selection process focuses on a whole variety of skills aimed at service to our customers. For instance, communication skills are very important. We think employees who have them will give us an advantage with our customers.

Sometimes customers themselves get involved in the process of hiring employees. For example, Southwest Airlines asks its Frequent Flyers to interview potential cabin attendants. This is a very powerful way to ensure that the employees hired are those who will excel at serving customers. Companies also rely on existing employees to determine if applicants will fit with the company's service culture.

We have a strong culture of service as opposed to self. We feel that service people have to be almost genetically predisposed to serve before they become really good service providers. It's a spirit of extending oneself for the customer. This applies at all levels within the bank. Our test for new hires: Would the person conducting the interview want to have the person over for dinner? Is there a comfort level? Will that person fit within the existing culture? We also don't have a personnel department. Each manager in the bank who has a set of customers—loan officer, deposit officer, and trust officer—is responsible for hiring, firing, and counseling employees. The message is clear. The managers who are responsible for customer satisfaction are also responsible for keeping employees focused on customer service.

GET THE WORD OUT

Employees need to be told about the organization's commitment to customers and how they are expected to fulfill it. Their motivation comes, in part, from understanding the organization's purpose, business, and position in the marketplace. They need to hear about management's commitment to customers, and they need to hear what customers think about it.

Glossy image brochures and newsletters, although they are still used, have increasingly been supplanted by communication methods that appeal to the MTV generation: videos, voice mail, pop-up computer screen messages, and TV call-in shows hosted by senior business executives. These venues provide management with the opportunity to update employees daily on customer satisfaction and financial goals.

The electronic media satisfy another requirement of employee communications: keeping employees as informed as customers. Industries as diverse as financial services and utilities know they must keep their employees one step ahead of the media. This example comes from a mutual fund company:

We want to be able to communicate urgent messages instantaneously to employees on their terminals. Today, employees are able to access only the company newsletter on-line. We want to be able to preempt their activity with an audio or visual signal. There's nothing more embarrassing than when customers know something before employees. With the speed of the media today, that can happen.

Ultimately, though, there is no substitute for personal communication. Employees need to be convinced that management is committed to serving customers. One company brought all its employees together for a weekend rally to make sure that they all heard the pro-customer message at the same time. This approach was so successful that the company holds these rallies every other year.

> *The first thing we did was to hold a kickoff rally over the weekend for all one thousand employees. At the rally we discussed statements that define the company culture. We talked about the need for care and concern for each other in order to have care and concern for clients. We introduced the concept of elegant service, which involves exceeding client expectations. When employees got back to their offices on Monday morning, there were cards on their desks introducing them to an elegant language. This consisted of seven phrases to use in customer calls such as "good-bye" instead of "bye-bye"—language that would set a professional image. The weekend became known as "Live the Spirit." To keep the spirit alive, every other year, we reconvene for another weekend. In addition, there are monthly seminars geared toward individual growth and development, on topics like Wellness and Volunteerism. "Live the Spirit" messages are also communicated daily via the voice-mail system.*

Other companies convene smaller meetings between senior executives and groups of employees. Here employees can say what's on their minds, and management can reply on the spot.

> *The CEO and other senior managers have lunch with every one of our three thousand employees in small groups*

annually. An employee's immediate manager is never part of the group—to encourage employees to speak their minds. And they do! Initially, the CEO found it very difficult to just listen and not defend everything. For issues that can't be resolved during the meeting, the CEO posts follow-up memos on company bulletin boards or on e-mail.

Even organizations with widespread, mobile employee populations such as airlines have found ways to communicate with their employees consistently. Although this airline has taken great advantage of voice mail, it also makes sure that senior managers meet employees personally:

Airlines have a challenge to communicate with a transient population of employees. We send voice-mail messages to every employee two or three times a week discussing customer service issues or overall company performance issues. The employees can call back on an 800 number and make comments, ask questions, or pass on rumors that can be addressed. But airline employees are no different from employees at other companies; they want to hear it from the "source." So management visits the larger stations once a month and the smaller stations once every two months. There is no set agenda; all questions are encouraged, and all topics are discussed.

This automobile manufacturer found it could communicate effectively with its many dealers through a dealers council. Creating the council helped to turn "many small companies into one big company":

We created a dealers council, which includes elected representatives from dealerships throughout the country. All issues are discussed with the dealers. They've been involved from the beginning, and it's made the whole process of getting closer to customers a lot easier.

Employees, for their part, need to internalize the organizational message, to understand what it means for their day-to-day activities. A bank told us how powerful this internalization can be:

Through policy management, we've established business priorities and driven them throughout the organization. Every employee, from the mail-room person to the president, knows what the key priorities of the business are and understands how their job aligns with those priorities. Our strength is the alignment. We have nine hundred employees going in one direction. That's very powerful.

REINFORCE THE CUSTOMER COMMITMENT

Organizations are changing constantly: New management teams form; new employees are hired, and new opportunities and threats arise in the marketplace. Under changing circumstances, it's easy for employees to forget about a company's commitment to serving its customers. Our research participants advise that management hold regular meetings with employees to keep their commitment to customers alive and uppermost in their minds. One company recommends one-on-one meetings between individual employees and senior management members:

Every eighteen months, each employee meets with a member of senior management for two hours. They discuss the state of the industry, competition, survivability, and personal concerns such as pay and benefits. However, the bulk of the dialogue focuses on how to improve the com-

pany. The meetings let employees vent their frustrations to someone in management; they also let management take action when appropriate. Even when a problem can't be resolved, it gives management the opportunity to give rational explanations such as why an employee can't have the perfect shift.

Another company recommends bringing together the stars of customer service to share best practices. This approach revitalizes the workforce and creates a network of problem solvers.

Every year, each subsidiary sends its best customer service teams to the company's world headquarters to share best practices. This event opens up an employee network for getting things done. It also avoids reinventing the wheel by letting employees leverage solutions from one geography to another. The employees return to their home countries excited about the company and the future, and their excitement spreads.

Another piece of advice from our research participants is to update employees continually. Here again, electronic communication has advantages:

When employees turn on their PCs in the morning, they see a video show updating them on customer and company performance issues. This way we avoid constantly bombarding employees with written information. Videos can also be released during the day on critical topics. The videos may take the place of staff meetings or impromptu meetings to discuss emergency situations.

EDUCATE TO SERVE

Our research shows that training is the number-one way that organizations focus their employees on serving customers (see Figure 5–1). Other methods include employee reward and recognition programs, teaming between employees or with customers, electronic or in-person communication, management directives, employee meetings, listening to customer feedback, and customer service competitions among employees.

With regard to training, some companies have given up on *classroom* training programs altogether. These programs, they feel, are geared either too high or too low, or else the information they deliver can't be put to use now if ever, or they cost too much. Instead, these companies now arm their employees with lists of skills needed for their jobs—things like selling or accounting skills. It's the responsibility of the employees to gain the skills that they don't have, or to enhance their present skills in order to perform their current jobs. Such companies offer

Figure 5–1   Methods Used to Focus Employees on Serving Customers

Note: multiple responses possible

training through computer-based programs or books, or else employees learn from their colleagues.

In addition to competency skills, such as sales or accounting, companies also encourage employees to develop customer focus skills. A typical employee curriculum would include the following subjects:

- organization values
- customer awareness
- customer values
- listening to customers
- root cause analysis
- process management
- customer empathy

The process of educating an employee starts on the first day on the job. The best way to begin is to discuss the values of the organization with the new employee. This way he or she learns what's most important to the company and can begin to understand his or her own role there.

Before benefits and insurance forms are discussed, we talk about the philosophy of the company. We talk about delighting customers. We talk about values. This way the employees understand why they're here. Then we talk about the mechanics: insurance benefits, vacation policy, and so on.

The educational process should be the same for all employees, our research participants caution. While the tendency is to emphasize frontline customer service employees, middle management should also hear and accept the message; otherwise they can become a formidable obstacle.

In the early days of our training initiative, we made a mistake. We left the supervisors, the first-line management, out. We went directly to the employees and started teaching them all new things and had them meeting as teams and solving problems. In many cases, there was no involvement or buy-in by direct supervisors, so there was a conflict. To some extent, the supervisors on the front line felt threatened. Once we realized the supervisors were not involved, we taught them the same things as the frontline employees: how to be team members, team leaders, and facilitators.

After the orientation session, some organizations find it helpful to provide a series of customer awareness classes. These classes teach employees and managers the value of customers to the organization and how to safeguard this very important asset.

We established a series of training programs to help change corporate culture. The first phase instructed managers on how to manage employees, the importance of quality, the way in which attention to the customer is important. The second phase emphasized that everybody is somebody's customer, no matter whether your customer is internal or external to the company. The third phase taught the facts of customer retention: the cost of losing a customer, the lifetime value of a customer, the cost of winning another customer versus the cost of being nice to a present customer. It really helped to have customers teach this section. The fourth phase focused on service recovery, empowering employees to right wrongs on the spot.

Even salespeople may well need customer focus training. One auto manufacturer videotaped customers testing its product in a competitive setting, then gave the videotape to each of its salespeople. The videotape showed the salespeople what customers think about the product when there are no salespeople around.

We brought a small focus group of customers to a test site, where they spent five hours comparing our new product with that of four competitors. The customers didn't know which car company was sponsoring the tests. The group inspected the features of each car, including warranties and pricing, and test-drove each vehicle. We videotaped the process and mailed the tape along with a workbook to our salespeople. We don't want our salespeople to use a sales spiel to sell the car. We don't want them to change the customer's mind. We want the process to lead the customer to a conclusion that they're happy with. That's what will last.

Typically, only a small percentage of a company's employees actually have regular direct contact with external customers. So it is particularly important to teach the other employees an awareness of their *internal* customers who ultimately serve external customers. Such training programs frequently use role-playing to help employees think about these customer relationships.

Every employee received two hours of training to help them identify at least one internal customer and one internal supplier. Then the employees met to discuss how they could work together. This helped sensitize employees to the importance of internal and then external customer needs.

As important as what is taught is who does the teaching. Star customer service performers and customers themselves make excellent "real-life" instructors. Small organizations have the luxury of using their CEOs as teachers.

Our CEO and his staff conduct employee training on customer service. This way the employees recognize that the company is serious about training, and serious about customers. It demonstrates real management "buy-in"—the company means what it says.

For employees who don't meet regularly with customers, many organizations find it helpful to make that opportunity periodically available. This may not involve their actually meeting customers, as one company explains; listening in on customer calls can be an equally effective technique:

Anybody who doesn't talk to customers every day is expected to listen to customer calls. They listen in order to understand what they can do differently in their jobs. What is it that the customers are asking us to do? What is it that they need? Then we ask the employees what they learned and what they're doing differently as a result.

Other companies prefer their employees to meet with customers directly, whether by phone or in person. This company's employees welcomed the opportunity to serve customers in its stores:

We offered all employees the opportunity to work in our stores two Saturdays in a row. The opportunity was well received; many more employees accepted the invitation than we anticipated. After the visits, their attitudes changed. They discovered they had a stronger sense of what they were working for—the company's products and its customers. Working in the stores helped them get to know the products better. "When you're representing your company on the shop floor, you want to be able to answer the customer's questions."

Once employees are sensitized to the importance of customers, they need to learn about the customers themselves. Who are they? What do they value? The organization must give them the information that will help them do their jobs. Some companies feel so strongly about customer values that they give customer focus training precedence over product training.

We completely redesigned our curriculum for new hires. The program used to consist of information on the company and its various products: "Here's Product A; here's how it works. Here's Product B, and here's how it works." Now the program is structured around: "Here are our customers, and here's how they think about their investments." Then: "Here are the products we have that will serve those needs." The original five-week program was expanded to twelve weeks to incorporate this new learning.

Technology is playing an increasingly important role in the education process. It can ensure that *all* employees understand what's important to customers.

Through distributed systems, we can make sure that employees have current information on customer satisfaction or customer complaints. This helps educate employees; it also helps them help customers. There are no excuses. The product development people can't claim that they never hear what customers are complaining about.

Some organizations give employees training to enhance their customer listening skills. Customer role-playing is used here as well:

We have our employees role-play customers. This enables discussions about what they think customers are saying and what the company should be doing. "I heard A, and you heard B. What did the customer really say, and what should we do?"

Monitoring the customer calls an employee handles is another way to teach customer listening skills:

Some employees listen to calls to coach the person taking the call. They remind them to listen to what the customer is saying, and to empathize with their situation. We want to be flexible in our responses—to make the solution match the customer's particular problem.

Even for employees who have regular customer contact, such as salespeople, many companies remind them to make time to listen to their customers. It's very easy for salespeople to assume that they know what their customers want, and to forget to ask them about their requirements from time to time.

As part of our training program for new representatives, customer contact is heavily emphasized. We have a household checkup program. We use that system to encourage our representatives to contact their customers on a regular basis to check their insurance situation, and find out what their current needs are.

Another goal of employee training programs is to develop a sense of organizational ownership among employees. Companies want employees who will take charge and fix things when something goes wrong, such as streamlining the complaints resolution process or shortening the delivery cycle. First, though, employees must be trained to identify what's gone wrong. This process is known as root cause analysis.

Identifying root causes in any system is key to problem solving and continuous improvement. Viewing problems as breakdowns in the system, root cause analysis examines the cause-and-effect chain of events that led to a problem. All possible causes are identified, and the root cause is finally found. Through this process, problems in the system can be discovered and solved. This approach is based on the assumption that accidents have multiple causes, that it is unproductive to blame employees, and that it is important to collect data before taking precipitous action. Critical to the success of this approach is reducing the fear of reprisal and educating all employees about the importance of system improvement. One company explains the importance of root cause analysis:

Employees need to identify the root cause of a customer's problem. Once they understand the root cause, it's a lot simpler to make the corrections required for a solution. Sometimes we send people on a mission to slay a dragon, and they can't even identify what the dragon looks like. Go out and kill something, we say. Sometimes this is good, but usually it's bad.

Employees also need to understand how the organization works so they can solve customers' problems. Often companies impart this knowledge by rotating employees among different departments throughout their careers. Another technique is cross-training, which educates employees about *every* service procedure so that they can substitute for absent employees or meet unexpected demand for certain services. One company felt that cross-training provided so many efficiency benefits that it made it the basis of its promotion plan:

We put in place a thirty-month advancement program for customer service representatives to reach "master level"—acquiring the skills necessary to work in every part of the customer service organization. The program boosted morale among the representatives; they wanted to get into training. The program also increased the efficiency of the customer service department. The master representatives were able to handle all types of customer calls, so they spent less time waiting for calls and more time answering customers' concerns.

Other organizations, like this bank, have made their problem-solving processes consistent across departments:

We educate all employees in the same methodology, which includes assessment, analysis, implementation, and ongoing management of the bank's business processes. The objective is that employees will be able to transfer their knowledge of processes from their experience in one project to a future project.

More than once, our research participants mentioned that they educate their employees about "processes" for fixing problems instead of about "procedures." Processes are less restrictive, giving employees the freedom to solve problems in the best way they can. Only companies that have given their employees the tools, education, and authority to solve problems can rely on process guidance.

We use process manuals, instead of procedural manuals, to help individuals understand their roles in delivering service to the customer. The employees understand that it is their job to determine how they fit into the process in a given situation, and they are empowered to add or eliminate steps anywhere they deem necessary. In one sense, the process is very well documented, but it's a process document; it doesn't explain what to do every day.

Last, but certainly not least, organizations are making an effort to teach their employees to empathize with customers— to identify with their individual circumstances, be flexible, and show they care. Empathy makes working with customers easier for employees and much more gratifying for customers.

Our customer-care training involves teaching employees to talk to customers in a different way, a more friendly way, and teaching them to listen more effectively. We're trying to get employees to stop thinking of customers as residential or business users and to start thinking of them as individuals, as people. This means flexing responses to meet individual needs and really listening. It requires being sensitive to many situations and responding accordingly, whether the customer is mad, elderly, doesn't hear well, or doesn't understand English. If associates really listen to customers, even if they have a serious problem, they can calm them down and provide an answer that relates to their situation. Sometimes it just pays to listen and take the beatings too! This is all about engendering some passion for customers.

DELEGATE AUTHORITY

Once employees have gained the necessary skills and understanding, organizations are more willing to give them the authority to fix processes or make apologies. This is known as employee empowerment. One research participant found that there are actually two types of empowerment: legislated and trust-based. True empowerment is trust-based.

Legislated empowerment stresses strict guidelines for employees to follow, almost demanding that employees fix something "or else." Trust-based empowerment focuses on developing employees' skills and attitudes by giving them the knowledge, training, support, and the right to resolve customer issues at the first point of contact. Legislated empowerment is restricting; trust-based empowerment is enabling.

Trust-based empowerment gives employees freedom to act on behalf of customers. Detailed rules and regulations are replaced with simple policy statements.

We use a policy sheet to provide guidelines on getting back to the customer. For example, if a customer calls about an issue, the policy is to respond to the customer right away—not within twenty-four hours. These guidelines are on just one piece of paper. They are laid out clearly and get updated when the standard gets revised. There are other policy papers concerning other areas of operations throughout the organization. The same approach has been applied, and it's been well received, precisely because they provide one clear, concise, easily distributed, and updated message.

Some companies have even developed simple ways for employees to revise processes outside of their particular departments.

Simplifying processes means faster resolution of customer problems.

All organizations in the company have a procedure whereby they can suggest changes to customer service processes, even if their organization doesn't own the process. Sometimes organizations use a monthly meeting; sometimes it's a form they fill out; sometimes they just tell their manager, who contacts the other organization. There's always a defined procedure.

Along with freedom, companies must also give employees the tools—the knowledge, ability, and authority—to serve customers. One company describes this mutually supportive arrangement as an "uncommon partnership":

We stress the "uncommon partnership." Maximum latitude is provided to individuals, while we supply information systems and measures of financial performance and customer satisfaction. The company provides the enablers and gives space to performers.

Empowerment, however, is a two-way street. If organizations are to give employees freedom and tools, employees have to want to take responsibility. Moreover, organizations have to make them feel comfortable doing it. The end result is employees whose self-esteem is so high that they *have* to take charge and fix problems.

Empowerment is not something that a firm can bestow upon employees; rather, it's something that employees have to want and take. The company's responsibility is to create an environment where processes are defined and

everyone is part of a process chart. Feedback from cus-
tomers dictates when processes need to be changed, and
it's the employees' responsibility to make the changes.

One company developed a very effective motto for communicating employee responsibility: "You see it, you hear it, you
own it."

Employees are trained to handle issues that come up. They
know who to get in touch with to resolve a customer's
problem. There are no hand-offs. You see it, you hear it,
you own it!

LEARNING BY DOING

If they were to do their customer focus initiatives over again,
some of our research participants said, they would spend less
time on training employees and get them involved in teams
much faster. Teams familiarize employees with what's important to customers, help bring the necessary resources to bear to
serve customers efficiently, and foster cooperation.

Some participants recommend putting people together in
natural work groups, rather than pulling them off to work on
things not related to their jobs. The smaller organizations tend
to rely on job-sharing programs, where employees spend three
months in every department getting to know how the organization works and becoming problem solvers. Many teams cross
functional boundaries, focus on processes, and direct their
activities without management aid. The result is more efficient
business processes.

Our key customer processes are defined as "order receipt
to billing." Self-directed work teams have been formed

*around these processes. The teams have created a tremen-
dous amount of synergy around people who were previously in different departments. The employees are learning
each other's jobs and doing a much more efficient job in
the hand-offs because together they're spotting problems
in the company's processes. Together they're now revising
or developing new processes to improve the overall work-
ings of the company.*

Teaming has other benefits as well. It creates a more capable
and pleasant work environment. People work together instead
of against each other. They work for customers instead of for
their bosses. They focus on fixing problems instead of blaming
individuals.

*Cross-functional teams have worked like magic to break
down the silo mentality at this company. Once the teams
start working toward a common goal, the walls start
breaking down. You can see it. You can see people making
phone calls instead of sending memos. You see people
dropping by to discuss issues. They focus on processes that
matter to customers. They run to the source of a problem
and determine how to change the process so it won't happen again. No individual is blamed.*

Teams have become a popular business practice as organizations struggle to develop learning organizations. Some of our
research participants have been using teams for many years.
One of them offers rules for successful teaming, based on their
experience:

*Rule 1: A representative of every function has to be on the
team and usually a supplier and customer. The customer
can be internal or external to the organization.*

Rule 2: Team members have to be involved in implementing the team's recommendations. This builds ownership.

Rule 3: Not everyone who is involved in the process can be represented on the team, so team members are required to discuss progress with their co-workers to create visibility and buy-in.

ORGANIZATIONAL STRUCTURES THAT SERVE CUSTOMERS

A reliance on cross-functional teams and a focus on improving business processes have caused some organizations to dismantle part of their traditional hierarchical organizational structures. One company chose to eliminate a layer of management on the shop floor. The result was that instead of management blaming employees, or vice versa, all production employees focused on creating more efficient processes.

We had one inspector for every twelve production employees. One day we eliminated the inspector title and made everyone a production employee. We made everyone responsible for their own work. As a result, product quality increased significantly. There was also a change in philosophy. Instead of management blaming employees, or employees blaming management, people started blaming the process. This eliminated fear, making it easier for people to take responsibility and make changes.

Another company replaced its hierarchical managers with process managers. It felt that no one manager could properly handle all the key processes—personnel development, client management, and revenue management—for a group of employees. The change helped streamline and improve the quality of decision making, which led ultimately to better customer service.

> *All functions are process managed. Instead of a manager being responsible for everything about a small group of employees, leaders are responsible for one specific process for a larger group of employees. The processes include career management and individual growth, client management, and revenue management. Process management is necessary, because one manager cannot simultaneously maintain each of these processes to a desired level. However, the process leaders do not operate in isolation. Close communication among the leaders is essential to their success.*

Organizations are also being restructured so that employees can spend more time with customers and less time doing administrative tasks.

> *As we talked to employees, we realized that sales managers and associates were spending only 20 percent of their time with customers and 80 percent of their time doing "back office" tasks. We set a goal of reversing that, so 80 percent of their time was spent on the sales floor. This change required an analysis of the salespeople's time to determine which tasks should be given to others. In fact, we relieved them of most of their nonsales duties. For example, they used to put stock in the back room on shelves and keep it straight and so forth. We created full-time replenishment teams. This was a major investment because it added payroll cost, but we felt we'd recoup the cost through increased business resulting from improved service. And we did.*

REWARD AND RECOGNIZE

Most of our research participants said that employee compensation programs should be structured to reinforce the organization's values. For example, in organizations with a strong team orientation, performance evaluations are conducted by team members—management, employees, and occasionally customers. Compensation, particularly bonuses, may also be team-based.

A few organizations take the idea of team compensation to an extreme. They eliminate all individual incentive compensation, such as management bonuses, sales incentives, and even team rewards. Instead, all employees are stock owners—when the company wins, everybody wins.

Most of the research participants tie employee compensation to customer satisfaction measures. Technology has made it easy for these organizations to track both individual and group performance. Here's one of the most detailed programs:

We measure over a hundred processes daily, things that we know are important in pleasing customers. For example, if a customer values responsiveness, we can measure how quickly the phone is answered; what percentage of calls are resolved before the call ends; and whether the customer service representative's terminal was available and how quickly the screens popped up. We set standards for each of these measures, and every day we report progress. If the standards are met, everyone receives a bonus. If they aren't met, then the money is accumulated. There are eight different ways for employees to keep track of performance. The results are posted in the cafeteria, and they can also be accessed on-line. We also change the measures frequently to reflect changes in customer values. It's a powerful way to keep people engaged in providing service to customers.

Another company developed a sales compensation system called the "repeat customer bonus," which encourages salespeople to develop long-term relationships with customers. Very simply, the salesperson who first sells to a customer gets a bonus on every subsequent sale made to that customer, regardless of whether it was made by that salesperson or even at that particular store. This system ensures that every customer who enters a store is treated the same way.

Our research participants also reward employees for suggestions that improve performance. Usually, the reward is a percentage of the savings or increased revenue generated by the suggestion. In an innovative approach, one organization encourages employees to turn suggestions into improvements:

Everyone who submits a suggestion receives one dollar. We value everyone's suggestion equally. The names of the persons who submit suggestions are placed in a hat. At the end of the month, one name is drawn. That person is entitled to a day off from work with pay. They can also nominate a senior manager to replace them on their day off. The amazing thing is that these people never take the day off when their substitute arrives. They keep an eye on them to make sure they don't make mistakes and jeopardize the team. Another interesting component of the program is that employees are required to follow through on their suggestions. This may require, for example, working with an engineer to develop and test a new part. The employees find this is a very rewarding experience.

Recognition, with or without reward, may be an even more powerful employee motivator. In fact, some employees clearly value recognition *more* than reward, particularly when it comes from their peers.

Our employee-to-employee recognition program is known as You Make the Difference. Employees send each other award certificates if they see someone exemplifying any of the company's values, which include trust, integrity, mutual respect, teamwork, continuous improvement, and the like. The certificates have a space for employees to sign their names and add a short note, which makes them easy for people to create and send. All levels of the company participate. The certificates can be redeemed for items from the company's gift catalogue. But most employees prefer to display the certificates in their work areas rather than redeem them.

Most organizations have lavish programs to recognize their top performers, the legends of customer service. World-class organizations also recognize the consistently good performers.

Every three months the high achievers, the people who really do "startling" things with customers, are made a fuss over by management—anointed as heroes. But the company also remembers to recognize the consistent performers, the people who always rank second or fifth in satisfying customers, the ones that seem to get customer bouquets consistently. The company has actually sensitized itself to look for these individuals and make sure they are recognized. Ultimately, both types of performers are role models. They give a very clear signal to employees about the type of attitude and behavior that the company admires.

It's important that *all* employees see management recognize special employees. These presentations can raise everyone's spirits and motivation; therefore, the bolder the demonstration the better:

> *We have a Power Award to recognize employees who delight internal or external customers. The award is a two-hundred-dollar check. Presentation is made in the area where the employee works. Management takes a bullhorn to the area and announces, "You did this for a customer. Thank you very much." It's a very special event. As an example, we recently recognized one of our installers. When he stopped working on Friday, he had just about finished a major installation. That weekend he played football and sprained his ankle. On Monday he was so concerned about the installation that he convinced his co-workers to take him to the customer site in a wheel-chair to complete the work. To say the least, the customer was impressed—and so were we!*

It is also important for an organization to recognize its suppliers and customers, since they are an integral part of its success. One company provided a very satisfying recognition experience for these individuals when it won the Malcolm Baldrige National Quality Award.

> *When we accepted the Malcolm Baldrige National Quality Award in Washington, D.C., in addition to twenty employees, we brought five customers and five suppliers with us. These were the people who helped us win. We never would have received the award without their support.*

Some organizations feel so strongly about making sure that employees are serving customers that they have eliminated special recognition altogether. Instead, they make recognition part of regular performance reviews.

Recognition is built into employees' regular performance reviews; it's nothing special. This way we make service part of every employee's daily work. Continuous improvement in work quality is an expectation from the organization rather than a nice "add-on." Employees have to improve their work; it's not optional.

Promotion can be a powerful form of recognition. With this strategy, though, an organization must be certain that the promotion rewards behavior that is important to customers.

The entry-level position in this company used to be the phone representative in customer service. No one wanted to be there, and we promoted the best representatives to management positions. However, after talking to our customers, we discovered that they wanted to talk to someone who was knowledgeable and could fix their problems. So we flipped the incentive system. The most knowledgeable managers are back on the phones, and the entry-level employees support them. We also improved their living conditions by giving them bigger cubicles with windows and better information systems. Now everyone wants to get back on the phones!

This company chose to create special positions to reward individuals who are particularly good at handling difficult customer issues:

We recognize individuals who have the ability to handle sensitive customer issues on behalf of senior management. They are known as executive action representatives. They are recognized by their peers and supervisors as competent individuals who can handle the tough cases.

MEASURE EMPLOYEE SATISFACTION
AND RETENTION

An organization should make sure its employees are satisfied with their jobs—satisfied employees create satisfied customers. The factors that create employee satisfaction, like customer satisfaction, change constantly. Therefore, the way employee satisfaction is measured must constantly be updated to reflect what's important to the employees.

Pay always seems to be the number-one issue affecting employee satisfaction. But after that, the priorities keep changing. One year it may be benefits, the next year working conditions. Priorities change because of the impact of "global" events like corporate restructurings or acquisitions. Sometimes we make progress on issues by responding to employee concerns highlighted in earlier surveys. It's amazing how much you can accomplish just by communicating with employees—clarifying the terms of their 401(k) program or benefits coverage can improve their satisfaction. It's important to be current about what's hot among employees and adjust the survey questions accordingly. Sometimes we even do focused surveys on issues that seem to be of particular concern to employees, like career progression or management attitudes.

Employee satisfaction surveys should always ask whether employees are satisfied with the organization's ability to meet and exceed customers' expectations. Is the organization providing the right products and services? Does it enable the employee to deliver superior service? What more needs to be done?

We use Dr. W. Edwards Deming's quality survey to ask employees what they think of the company's performance.

We ask them to evaluate the company against every one of Deming's fourteen points. This includes how well we're teaching and instituting leadership, creating a climate for innovation, and facilitating pride of workmanship. This process has produced great results. The more the firm educates employees, the tougher they get on Deming's points. In effect, the matrix is changing constantly. Even when the results show no improvement, it's because the employees' expectations increase every year.

Figure 5–2 shows that almost half of our research participants conduct employee surveys at least annually.

After a survey is completed, organizations should share the results with employees and take action as quickly as possible to rectify employee complaints. Surveying employee satisfaction is no different from surveying customer satisfaction. In fact, some of our research participants use very similar tools for both employee and customer surveys.

Figure 5–2   **Frequency of Employee Surveys**

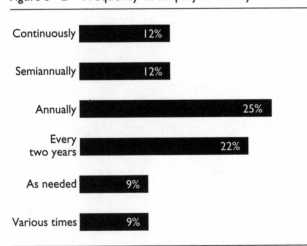

Note: multiple responses possible

We conduct two types of employee surveys. One, done by an outside firm, measures employee satisfaction at competing firms in our industry. The results provide benchmarks. The other is a monthly survey of every employee to find out what's working or not working. The same telephone technique used for customers is used for employees. Hey, if we're talking to our customers every day, we should be talking to our employees every day. It's a quick interview, takes less than five minutes, and the results are reported to all employees monthly.

In addition to employee surveys, organizations also find it useful to benchmark employee satisfaction and retention rates against those of similar companies. Regular benchmarking can identify areas of employee dissatisfaction.

We frequently benchmark employee retention rates against our competitors. The results compare very favorably, and we attribute this to the benchmarking process itself. Benchmarking highlights sources of employee dissatisfaction so we can quickly be on top of them and take the proper steps to rectify the situation. We feel very strongly about the need for monitoring retention because of the tremendous resources we invest in employee recruitment and especially training and education.

Finally, the research participants emphasized the importance of making the customer focus initiative fun for employees. This aids the employee retention effort.

Celebrate the initiative a lot so people see it's fun in addition to work. But don't get too corny and rah-rah about it, because people get burned out and bored with that pretty fast. You have to make it fun but not frivolous. That's hard to do when you're talking about something as ephemeral as quality and service.

CREATE THE PASSION!

Customer focus is a balance between art and science. The scientific part is the measurement systems. They're absolutely necessary. Without them an organization doesn't know where it's been or where it's going. Are its employees and customers more or less satisfied? Art is the other piece. No employee can really be taught to care about customers. But no company can be truly customer-focused without employees who are passionate about customers.

Passion. You've got to have passion, or it won't happen. The employees have to believe. We're just starting to hear the stories about customer service heroes, such as the people who helped clients during a hurricane. You hear those stories so frequently, it's like a myth. They help make everybody aspire to do well.

At best, companies can provide an environment and a set of tools for employees that make caring possible. Then keep at it!

There's an art to customer focus—associates who have the right tone with customers, who have a helpful attitude, who have the will to listen intently to what somebody says and then act on it, who find new ways to deliver. We find new ways every day. Yesterday we had ninety-two suggestions from employees. This month we'll have probably 2,400 suggestions from a target audience of fewer than 2,000. We keep finding new ways to do things better, and better, and better.

SOUND ADVICE

All employees, at every level of the organization—those who serve internal as well as external customers—are responsible for implementing the organization's customer focus initiative. Employees are the ones who make it happen.

Getting employees to do their job well requires much more than just telling them. It requires establishing a standard, formal or informal, to hire individuals who want to delight customers. Then employees must be educated to understand and serve customers; they must be given the authority to make decisions on behalf of customers; and they must be recognized and rewarded when they do the right things. The investment is psychic as well as financial. Everybody has to be encouraged to care about customers and should enjoy doing it.

6

Developing and Delivering Pro-Customer Service

EMPLOYEES WHO ARE TRULY PRO-CUSTOMER provide consistently good service. In every industry, customers today are demanding better service from the companies with which they do business. They are more likely to switch suppliers because of poor service than poor quality or expensive products. As we saw in Chapter 4, companies that recognize how important service is to their customers segment their customers according to their service requirements.

In the past, customer service was the responsibility of a separate organization that supported the customer primarily after the sale. Today, customer service is every employee's responsibility and is as likely to occur before or during the sale as it is after the sale.

Service is also likely to be integrated with every product a company offers. For example, grocery stores now offer shopping services for busy customers, allowing them to fax in their orders and receive home delivery. Automotive companies have expanded their service plans with more services such as courtesy transportation, longer hours, and a lifetime warranty on parts and labor. One of our research participants uses a variety of means to add service to its products:

Our plan has been to create a position that's sufficiently attractive to justify a higher—though still reasonable—price. We do this by adding value—through convenience, reputation, promotions, and last but not least, service.

A bank relies upon the "extra touches," unrelated to its products, to build a special bond with customers:

For years, we've been offering things like free shoe shines or local produce to our customers in addition to an ever-changing array of banking services to meet their needs. What we've found is that the extra touches help build the relationship with the customer. We've changed customers' expectations to the point where they think of us almost as a club. That's an important distinction: "customer" is a bit distant; "member" is a bit more possessive.

Other companies have adopted the service standards of world-class companies such as Federal Express and Ritz-Carlton Hotels because their customers have come to expect such exemplary treatment. This bank chose L.L. Bean as a role model:

We wanted to become the L.L. Bean of banking, so we developed a twenty-four-hour sales and service group so customers could contact the bank from home or office any time of the day or night. We also developed a "services at a glance" catalog providing detailed descriptions of the services offered by our customer service center.

Other organizations, like this airline, have transformed their products into total service experiences:

Through market research studies, we learned that airline passengers judge satisfaction as more than satisfaction

*with the aircraft seat. They evaluate the whole service,
from flexibility in making reservations through to arrival
at a hotel. In response, we offer check-in by telephone
for passengers carrying only hand luggage. We have up-
graded facilities such as our arrivals lounge, which now
offers shower facilities, meals, and phones. We also make
chauffeur-driven rental cars available to take passengers to
their final destination.*

The challenge most organizations face, given that service has
become so important and omnipresent, is to make their services
unique. In this chapter, we'll review how our research participants use segmentation strategies, information, delivery practices, service recovery procedures, and employee performance
to differentiate their offerings.

SERVICE SEGMENTS

The starting point for creating unique services is to understand
what customers value. One bank, beset by the overuse of the
term *customer service* in its industry, has tackled this problem
innovatively:

*Several other industries had created products and services
that became financial services. Recognizing this situation,
upper management determined that superior customer service was the best way to retain customers who might be
lost. One problem with this strategy was that the term* customer service *has always been used in the banking industry. To try and make it something different from what the
customer knew was difficult. Managing the change is very
delicate but very important. We spent a lot of time meeting
with customers and talking to customers who had closed
their accounts with us to understand what they meant by*

customer service. Clearly for us it was a strategy not only to increase profitability by retaining customers but also to survive.

Unfortunately, many companies add layers of services to their offerings without considering customers' individual needs. They usually offer more services than customers want, at prices that reflect neither their value to the customers nor the cost of providing them. Many companies don't know which services customers with similar needs really want; nor do they understand which services should be part of a standard package and which can be offered as options. Salespeople too often give away services to win a deal, even if profitability is reduced.

All too often, our company gives away optional services at the end of the year to meet sales quotas. In fact, I'm not even sure that our salespeople always know which services are standard and which are optional; they're too focused on winning the deal. They also confuse customers' expectations about what's standard and what's optional. For example, our cost-reduction studies are optional services. A company review, however, revealed that our top customer always seemed to get this service for free.

This approach to service can be very expensive, as one company found out:

We invested a lot of money opening a twenty-four-hour-a-day customer service center in Japan, a service that was a big hit in the United States. But when we surveyed our Japanese customers about their service preferences, the center ranked seventh. Surprisingly, but not so in hindsight, the number-one preference was to increase the number of golf courses that would accept our credit card.

Some companies are realizing that they can provide services at a lower cost yet still meet customers' needs more effectively, gain more business, and enhance profits. They build flexibility into their service offerings. They start by defining the minimum level of services that all customers in a given segment uniformly value and then sell those services at the lowest price that will yield a profit. Options are added to meet the needs of individual customers within the segment. In this way, they can more easily retain and expand business with their most valuable customers. One of our research participants does it this way:

We divide our customers into two categories: strategic (those that have committed themselves in contracts to building a broad, long-term relationship with us) and transactional (those that do business with us on an order-by-order basis). We focus our services on helping our strategic customers to improve their services and financial performance. Even services offered as options are carefully designed to provide value or savings that far exceed their cost. To do this, we spend time up front with clients to prepare a set of mutually defined metrics for determining the value of our work to the client. As a condition for working with us, the client must agree to apply these measures and document the results. This way we get a concrete idea of the value of our work. When we know the benefits of our services, we also have a much easier time winning over new clients.

SERVICE IS INFORMATION

The process of instituting unique customer services starts with needs-based segmentation. Then a company must look to best practices in service content, delivery, and recovery to ensure that its services are top quality. One best practice is to view providing information as a service. Customers are eager to learn more about the organizations with which they do or might do business, to help them make purchase decisions. They often want to know everything about a company—its products, its employees, and its other customers.

Providing to customers information that was formerly held confidential is now considered a customer service. About 70 percent of our research participants make such information available to their customers electronically. Figure 6–1 shows the types of information that the research participants are willing to share with their customers on-line.

Eight percent of the participants claim that they provide "everything" that their customers request, but the vast majority are more cautious. About 40 percent provide order to billing data, which include information about product availability, order entry, delivery schedules, billing procedures, and order-tracking mechanisms. Customers can also view information about their accounts such as product/service histories, satisfaction ratings, and the status of current orders. On-line product

Figure 6– 1   Information Customers Can Get On-Line

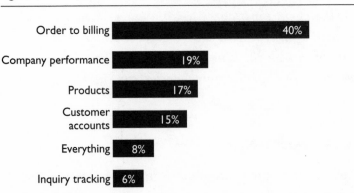

Note: multiple responses possible

and pricing catalogs are also becoming more popular. A few companies are enabling their customers to interact in the service process, so they can track the status of their inquiries or complaints on-line.

Customers can check rates and current product information. If the tax laws change, we can provide advice on-line for them to decide among available alternatives. They can monitor changes in their account balances electronically. A feedback mechanism enables them to ask questions or make complaints. Customers get individual responses, but we can also make the answers to more general questions and complaints available for all to see. Of course, a personal representative is always available to answer any additional questions the system doesn't accommodate.

Providing information to customers electronically is part of a concerted effort companies are making to educate their customers. Educated customers know what type of service to expect, and they can either avoid problems (given that 20–40 percent of customer problems are caused by the customers themselves) or solve their own. A little education up front can go a long way to improve service.

Some companies are using their marketing communications activities to tailor their educational, consultative service approach to individual customer needs. One investment company uses traditional and innovative communications techniques to educate its customers:

For a variety of reasons, ranging from changes in the economy to the shift from defined benefit plans to defined contribution plans, investors are taking more accountability for their financial futures. Our marketing communications efforts attempt to separate what is nice to know from what investors need to know to plan appropriately for investment objectives. While we still advertise in core business publications, we have significantly expanded our communications channels in our effort to reach more people. This includes using infomercials, teleseminars, in-flight programs, and magazines geared toward individual investors, 401(k) plan participants, and retirees. Workbooks are also geared toward active investors, helping them to evaluate an existing portfolio, and novice investors who need assistance in developing investment goals and allocations.

Providing customer service means getting the right information to the right customers. Many organizations now use their service-need segmentation strategy to tailor customer mailings. They may send out specialty catalogs that are further customized with bound-in promotional offers and personalized messages printed on the wraps. Such a message might thank a customer for her recent purchase or recognize the anniversary of a longtime customer. In the age of junk mail, this approach not only makes the customer happy, it also saves money for the company.

Some organizations use their customer newsletters to provide information that is unrelated to the organization but that customers still are glad to have:

Our monthly newsletter isn't your typical bank newsletter. Last month, we gave readers advice on the best time to view the whales off the California coast. When the local classical music station changed to an all-news format, we let readers know that they could listen to a New York station on cable three hours every evening.

Information flow should be two-way. Organizations must make it easy for customers not only to obtain service but also to communicate their service requirements. Electronic communication simplifies and speeds the flow, as for this manufacturer:

A customer can query an order status. A customer can enter an order automatically for standard product. A customer can enter an order automatically for custom product by being on-line with the design department. Complaints can be entered on-line and the status of the resolution viewed. Customers can talk to the billing department about payment status. Information availability has done a lot to increase customer satisfaction. I don't know a part of the company that doesn't enable the customer to access their information systems. We'll even sell them the telecommunications services to help them do it.

The same manufacturer has future plans for electronic communication:

By the year 2000, our customers are going to know everything about us: yields in manufacturing, run times, cycle times, and so on. All commerce will be done on-line, including funds transfers. Video conferencing will replace travel. Phones will be equipped with video screens to humanize the process.

Technology enables two-way communication to take place in some unlikely ways. Not surprisingly, it is provided in places where customers need service the most. One airline is planning interactive communication in-flight:

We're looking into providing passengers an interactive capability to enable them to make inquiries about flight status in-flight. It might be a kiosk on the airplane or screens in the seatbacks. The purpose is to give passengers a little more control over their flight agenda. They could ask: Where is the airplane? How long is it going to take to get to the destination? Will the flight arrive on time or how late/early? If late, what alternative connecting flights are available? We'll also use this technology to enable customers to log complaints, for example, about bad meals. The sooner we know there is a problem, the sooner we can fix it.

An electric utility sees possibilities in interactive electric meters:

It would be great to be able to give customers real-time information through their electric meters about electric usage or power outages. We could provide information about real-time pricing as an alternative to historical fixed pricing. Or in the event of a power outage, we could inform customers when their power will be restored. This would keep the customer current and clear the phone lines for emergency calls. In addition, customers could use the system to communicate local problems or make inquiries.

Since services are so heavily provided these days and since many services are hidden as product add-ons, organizations are finding it well worth the effort to remind customers of the value of the services they've delivered. Discount warehouse clubs have been doing this for years. At the end of each sales receipt, they promote their buying services by emphasizing customer savings: "By shopping with us today, you saved $50.00 off retail prices." Other organizations, such as this computer company, are recognizing the value of this new type of informational service:

Every year for every customer, we establish a plan and together decide what it's going to take to keep the customer as satisfied as possible. Part of the plan includes an outline of the free services we will make available, such as seminars and product performance evaluations. At the end of the year, as part of the annual progress summary, we make sure we remind the customer how many seminars and product evaluations were conducted and what their impact was on the customer's bottom line.

SERVICE DELIVERY

Companies are reexamining not only the types of customer service provided but how the service is delivered. So important has service become that many companies are trying to "industrialize" elements of it, to make service more tangible to customers. A very simple example is in the cleaning of hotel rooms. Maintenance workers now fold toilet tissue into a *V* to indicate that the room has been cleaned.

Organizations are also taking a hard look at the quality of their service procedures. Do they meet customer requirements? Are they providing service in a timely fashion? How can we reduce the number of hand-offs and make sure the customer is communicating with the person who can help them? Are the customers happy with the result? Are we providing service in the most cost-efficient manner? One company redesigned its service processes based on their answers to those questions.

For every service process that we think needs to be redesigned, we do a customer value analysis. That's part of the team's job. Three metrics are involved. The first is improvement in customer value. The redesigned process should add significant customer value, according to the customer, or why do it. We shoot for 50 percent improvement. The second metric is cycle time. Faster is better. Less time is better service. The goal is a 50 percent reduction in cycle time. The third metric is cost. We expect a 33 percent reduction. Of the three, the one that really drives improvement is cycle time. Challenge the team to cut the time in half, and that really forces innovation. They strip the process down to its essentials.

Some companies are trying to control the variability in their employees' service performance. They want to keep their employees focused on making a sympathetic connection with customers, rather than worry so much about the specific elements of service. This approach can even be applied to something as mundane as cleaning hospital rooms. One janitorial services company defined an easy-to-follow seven-step process for room cleaning. In step one, the janitor cheerfully greets the patient; in step seven, he asks the patient if there is anything else they might need. These two steps are crucial to establishing a sympathetic connection, yet the company is also arming its employees with the skills, facts, and authority necessary to properly serve customers.

The increasing complexity of service delivery processes has encouraged many companies to use teams of employees to serve customers. Teams can bring to bear immediately the resources necessary to meet and exceed customer expectations. Teaming also appeals to customers' demand for one-stop service.

We created self-directed, cross-functional work teams to service clients who tend to have a variety of products. The teams developed as a result of past situations where a client had to call up to ten different organizations to get answers involving different products. The client teams, numbering between ten and twenty employees, come from all different product and service areas in the company. They own the customer; they report to the customer and are measured by the customer.

Some organizations create cross-functional teams that can service front-line employees. As one research participant said, "Nothing that really matters to the excellence of the organization can really be solved in one department."

We created a parallel organization that supports the customer service and sales organizations. The organization is known as the Critical Resource Team. It includes individuals from sales planning, accounts receivable, credit, distribution, warehousing, and market research. They serve in an advisory capacity, providing information to the front-line personnel in response to customer inquiries. They're our "one-stop shop." They're also part-time marketers; from time to time they may be called on to interface with customers.

One universal need to which companies are increasingly responding is the need for convenience, especially the convenience of self-service. More and more customers are now serving themselves. Gas stations and banks were early proponents of self-service, but fast-food restaurants, brokerage firms, and airlines have been quick to follow. Levi Strauss became famous for its Personal Pair service. The PC-based systems it installed in its retail stores allow customers to design jeans to their own specifications rather than take them off the rack. The customer-generated specifications are transmitted to Levi's plants, where the custom jeans are produced along with standard Levi's. Other companies have followed suit: For example, hardware stores now provide kiosks where customers can design bathrooms and kitchens.

One bank that participated in our research opened a telephone sales and service center that fields calls twenty-four hours a day, seven days a week. This self-service strategy has been very successful in winning over new customers:

Customers can bank from their home, office, or even their car. This service helped us triple the number of new accounts opened over the prior year. Next year we're looking to open the "branch of the future." It will operate in a shopping mall, be open twenty-four hours a day, and rely primarily on ATMs and video terminals that connect the customers with service representatives. We might have a live branch officer present.

FAST, COORDINATED RECOVERY

No matter how well an organization designs its products and services, it will receive complaints. Frankly, very few dissatisfied customers actually complain. For the most part, companies have no idea why their customers leave them. The problem is compounded by the fact that dissatisfied customers most likely do tell their friends and relatives of their displeasure. Smart companies recognize the value of complaints. They make it easy for their customers to complain, and they try to resolve their problems as quickly and fairly as possible.

Complaints themselves are an excellent performance measure. Their frequency and their content indicate when an organization has lost touch with its customers, and what it may need to do to get back on track. Complaints can be a gold mine of information about how to improve business performance.

Like customers, not all complaints are created equal. Most companies prioritize which customer complaints they respond to by their frequency—the more often a problem occurs, the more likely it is that a company will spend money to fix it. But the most common complaints are not necessarily the ones that point to the biggest problems. One airline that participated in our research found that half of its customers had experienced one or more problems, most frequently long waits, flight delays, poor meal quality, uncomfortable seating, and unclean toilet facilities. The airline was surprised that its customers considered unclean toilet facilities and meal quality to be the most serious problems. While it seems sensible to spend money to improve all these product or service areas, the airline realized greater profit improvement faster by initially concentrating on those two most damaging areas.

From the customer's standpoint, the speed of response to a complaint counts for almost as much as the content of the response. In today's fast-paced world, rapid response time is becoming a hallmark of care. One credit card company changed its operations and measurement systems to accommodate this trend:

Customers want the complete answer to their question before they hang up the phone. They don't want the company to call back. They don't want a letter next week. They don't want a note on their bill. Once we recognized how important this was to customers, we started measuring how fast we answer the phone and what percentage of customer questions were answered on the first call. In the beginning, only 60 percent were answered on the first call. Then we started raising the bar. Today we're answering 95 percent of questions on the first call. This is very different from the way we used to measure responsiveness.

We used to measure the length of the call, believing that shorter calls were more responsive. Our customers told us this wasn't necessarily true. A shorter call often required a callback. So today we don't measure the length of the phone call. We want the representatives to spend as much time as necessary listening to customers and responding to their concerns on the first call.

Advances in technology have enhanced the speed and responsiveness of complaint resolution. Computer systems that record customer complaints and route them for resolution ensure that action will be taken. With such systems, issues can't fall between organizations, and phone representatives can't hide if they've been rude to a customer. Systems that enable customers to enter complaints directly into a database can also save time. Often these systems allow customers to view how similar complaints were resolved, thereby further accelerating the process.

Efforts are also being made to integrate telephone and computer technology to improve service. For example, automatic number identification (ANI), which is now available on many customer information systems, enables service representatives to identify callers and access their profiles as soon as a call is picked up. This means that representatives can spend their time listening to customers' concerns instead of searching for their account information. Another integrative technology, information indicator digits, indicates the type of phone a caller is using, such as a hotel/motel phone, a coin phone, or a cellular phone. Clever use of these digits can single out customers with particular needs. For example, a travel agency can target callers from pay phones for high-priority routing to agents specializing in changes in itineraries.

Applications such as skills-based routing and call vectoring can also improve call handling. In skills-based routing each agent is assigned a certain area of expertise, such as product-line knowledge, transaction-type abilities, or individual customer acquaintance. Vectoring routes a call to the agent who has the appropriate skills to handle it. Using these applications, a travel agency can route its top clients to their preferred travel consultants or to designated backup consultants.

Voice-recording units (VRUs) make it easier for service representatives to record customer comments and complaints after a call is completed. Careful analysis of VRU data helps companies to track complaints, recognize patterns, and develop solutions faster. A credit card company uses VRUs this way:

After customer service representatives hang up from a customer call, they access a voice-recording unit and tell the system exactly what the customer just told them. At the end of the day, the customer comments are downloaded into a database. A weekly report is published summarizing the top five customer issues found in the database. Customized versions of the report are sent to fifty internal departments, covering the key areas for which they are responsible. The departments then have the responsibility to respond to the customers' concerns.

When a caller's question can't be answered immediately, companies often search their databases and use outside sources of information to help them estimate the response times. An investment company goes to such lengths to assist its customers:

If an answer to a customer's question requires research, we quote how long that type of research takes instead of a standard cycle time. Daily, we track how long it takes to resolve different types of problems. For example, based on current volumes, an incorrect posting to your account will be resolved in two days. We're also trying to figure out how we can track current mail-delivery times.

Responsiveness also increases when customer service representatives have easy access to product and other information. Such access enables them to answer a broad range of customer questions quickly and easily. Companies are also giving their sales teams access to the same information through their PCs, so that they can respond to customers' issues on site. About 93 percent of our research participants provide information to their *employees* electronically—a much higher proportion than the 70 percent who provide information to their *customers* electronically.

Figure 6–2 describes the types of information that the research participants share with their employees. Compared to Figure 6–1, which shows the information they make available to their customers, it's apparent that they share more information with their employees than with their customers.

Figure 6–2   Information Employees Can Get On-Line

Note: multiple responses possible

Technology is key to sorting out this fast-growing mountain of information. Very few employees can keep track any longer of all the information that their customers may request. Information systems store the necessary information, freeing service representatives to listen to their customers. For this company, technology is playing a key role in enabling its customer service representatives:

The phone representatives have ready access to all kinds of information: product specifications, service records, customer satisfaction results, complaint logs, customer solutions, and current order, delivery, and service time frames. If we think it will help customers, we make it available in the system. The system is there to maintain the facts; we want the representatives to be listening to the customers and figuring out how they can help them.

Our research participants did offer some advice about one type of information—customer account data. This information should be used to serve the customer's needs as well as the company's marketing needs cautiously. As one participant said, "There's nothing worse than a telemarketer who calls and says, 'We know you have a child who's twelve years old.'" Nevertheless, customers do expect marketers to know a great deal about them, at least enough about how they live and do business to be able to zero in and tell them how a product or service fits their specific needs. Today, companies must carefully walk a very fine line between customer knowledge and invasion of privacy.

The increasing amount of information available to employees has to be structured in a way that helps employees find answers to customer questions quickly. Such structuring can be better developed, as one participant explains, when employees participate in the design of their computer systems:

The customer information system used to be structured with a tree index. There were initially sixteen options for the representative to choose from, then fourteen choices within each of those categories. The problem was it took too long for the representative to get to the right information, and if they made a mistake, they had to put the customer on hold and start all over again. Because of these problems, the representatives are very involved in the system redesign. In fact, the new system is being designed around how the representative thinks about how to answer the customer's question. The object is to try to short-circuit the cycle, so the right information is obtained as quickly as possible.

Technology can speed the complaint-resolution process, but sometimes the process must be entirely redesigned in order to be effective. One company pared its thirteen-step complaint-resolution process down to a mere five steps: listen, apologize, express concern, make amends, and record the event. In addition, it taught employees to use their judgment to determine how best to respond to a customer rather than to escalate the issue to management. In general, these changes enabled employees to answer complaints in half the time that was required before. Other companies have also recognized the need to make it easy for their customers to complain, so they locate complaint desks in visible places or list toll-free phone numbers on their products.

Still other organizations are working to skip the complaint process altogether. A software company notified its dealers about bugs in its current product and offered them compensation for any lost business or damaged customer relations. The company's proactive stance ensured that very few dealers accepted the offer.

Customers prefer to have their problems solved not only quickly but by one person. When employees have all the information they need to solve customers' problems, it becomes possible. But it also requires employees to accept responsibility for the resolution process. Some companies have found it necessary to encourage their employees to take action. For example, they permit their employees to spend certain amounts of money to resolve customer problems as they see fit:

> *All employees are trained so that if a phone rings any-where and they're walking by, they pick it up and say, "Yes, I can help you." We back that up by giving every employee a thousand dollars to spend on customer service, no questions asked. For example, they can spend the money to replace defective products or expedite product deliveries. We even changed the name of customer com-plaints to customer action requests to encourage employ-ees to be responsive.*

Another company, an airline, created new positions in which employees would have primary responsibility for resolving customer problems in their functional areas:

> *We created positions known as lead flight attendant, lead station attendant, and lead passenger aide. These people have primary responsibility for service in their areas, whether on the ground or in the air. The leadership roles help give employees a sense that they are in control; they have the authority to solve customer problems.*

Organizational restructuring may be necessary to make such single-point resolution possible. For example, companies that have disparate product groups sometimes create a single service organization that is knowledgeable about and able to support all products. That way, the dissatisfied customer has to make only one call instead of many. Other companies have a customer service organization that reports directly to senior management, instead of one that is part of the sales or marketing department. This structure makes it easier for the customer service organization to resolve disputes between departments. One research participant chose to create a customer relations position that reported directly to senior management.

> *We created a customer relations position to make sure that we understand what customers need and can respond quickly to their requests. This person reviews all the customer complaints received by senior management; uncovers whether or not there is a systemic problem within the company; and then works with senior management to fix it. Even if there are perception problems—for example, if a customer feels she has been treated rudely—senior management will address the issue. With the chairman's active support, this person also gets departments to work together to solve problems. We want to avoid the parochial view of departments examining in isolation how they provide customer service. All in all, the customer relations position has helped us solve customer complaints "first and fast."*

One way organizations can make the complaint-resolution process easier is to offer service guarantees to customers. That way, customers know what to expect, and employees know what will satisfy them. One company guaranteed that it would donate fifty dollars to a national charity whenever a service representative failed to meet a commitment, such as delivering a product on time. This method helped the company track and measure employee performance, and it has also become the basis of the company's learning system.

It has focused the entire organization on customer service. The standards of success are unambiguous; it will cost us fifty dollars if the guarantee is invoked. The guarantee also generates feedback. It helps us isolate customer problems and develop solutions, hopefully before the problems get out of hand. And it increases customer satisfaction, making our customers even more loyal, active marketers for our company. Fifty dollars is a small price to pay to improve the performance of our company.

As one company found out, such guarantees work only if employees are capable of carrying out the service in the first place. If not, they can be very expensive:

We used to give customers promises, but once we saw that we could keep the promises fairly easily, we gave them guarantees. The guarantees relate to delivery time and repair service. We also follow up with all customers to see if they are satisfied. In the event of a guarantee failure, customers are credited with a quarterly rebate or up to three quarterly rebates if service is really bad. The credit responsibility is at the front line. The representatives have the authority to give the customer credit without asking a manager.

SERVICE TO A "T"

Customers expect organizations to respond to their concerns with flexibility. They want to be treated as individuals, whether they are frequent buyers or complainers. "Standard policy" is not good enough anymore. Knowledgeable employees who have more authority, smaller groups of employees who are closer to customers, and management support are all prerequisites for flexible response. One organization even found it necessary to institute flexibility training:

We bring together a team of people from sales and invoicing, field technicians, and product experts to discuss how they can improve service. In particular, this approach will be used to train field technicians as customer service representatives. We want to give the field technicians the latitude to provide superior service, such as adjusting an invoice if service wasn't provided as promised.

Still, it's doubtful that any company will ever build a perfect customer service delivery system. Systems and people are imperfect, and aligning their competencies with every customer's perception of excellent service will never happen. Instead, some companies now encourage their customer service representatives to establish a dialogue with each customer to understand what their expectations are for that transaction and how the company can satisfy them. This process is not about establishing a standard for handling the average customer; it's not even about establishing a standard for the majority of customers. It's about establishing a standard for each customer. It's customized customer service.

It's not designed to meet all the customer's needs. Instead, it focuses on understanding customer expectations and then meeting our commitments to them. For example, if a customer calls to complain about a rate increase, we explain what the representative can do and how the customer too can contribute to an improved outcome. Many times we can't change the price of our products, but the customer can get a full, truthful, and honest explanation of the cause of the increase. Remember, our objective is to satisfy our customer once we have explained what's possible.

Our research participants encouraged their employees to empathize with customers—or as one company said, to "stand alongside angry customers." Empathizing with customers can smooth the complaint-resolution process and help build loyal customers. Knowledgeable customer service representatives may actually be the most empathetic, since they are most likely to be able to solve the customer's problem.

We've stayed away from the "smile and dial" training sessions that show employees how to listen to, probe, and respond to complaints. These programs tend to produce behavior that customers feel is phony. Instead, we cross-train employees to increase their abilities to solve customer problems on their own. The most empathetic response is a solution to the customer's problem.

Sometimes it makes sense to involve the customer directly in the complaint-resolution process, as this airline does:

We run a "come fly with me" program. If a customer calls with a baggage problem, we send a staff person with him on his next flight, to see the process from check-in to baggage claim through the customer's eyes. We take him behind the scenes and show him the baggage hall. At the same time, seeing things from the customer's viewpoint, we learn what needs to be fixed.

Employee performance measures may have to be revised in order to change employee behavior. One company, instead of emphasizing complaint reduction, now rewards employees who help bring hidden problems to the surface.

Finally, companies caution, don't forget to apologize! Some companies empower their employees to give gifts to customers as a form of apology.

If I'm checking you in, and I really mess something up (which happens every so often), I'm empowered to send you a small gift as an apology. The customers often write back and thank us and say they are a customer for life.

SOUND ADVICE

Customer service has become such an important competitive differentiator that it is no longer solely the responsibility of a small group of individuals staffing a complaint desk. Customer service is every employee's responsibility, and it should be a proactive rather than a reactive strategy. Excellent service wins and keeps customers.

Service means extras—product, care, and information—customized to meet the similar needs of a group of customers. Service has become so complex and inclusive, extending from order planning to postsales service, that a cross-functional team of employees is often needed for service delivery.

Some things haven't changed. The three F's of service still apply. It has to be fast, flexible, and come from the first person contacted. Only today, the first person may be a computer, and fast means instantaneous.

7

Retaining Existing Customers

BY NOW, the reasons companies should try to retain customers are clear. It costs much less, up to five times less, to retain an existing customer than it does to acquire a new one. Revenue and profits increase as customers stay with a company. Long-term customers can provide not only financial rewards but "knowledge rewards," helping the company understand how it can improve performance. Last, but certainly not least, *customers* themselves are demanding individualized attention from and long-term relationships with their suppliers. Not every customer, to be sure: Some customers don't want relationships with their suppliers, and most companies don't want relationships with each of their customers. Rather, customer retention efforts are focused typically on high-value customers.

Customer retention is really relationship-building. It doesn't just happen. Organizations go through a process, probably transparent to most, to build relationships and retain customers. This chapter describes that process.

Today, many organizations are talking about establishing relationship-type marketing strategies, or else they have already done so. Such strategies require rethinking the customer relationship and expanding it from a series of independent transactions to an interdependency, where mutual interests and needs are addressed. A bank shows what this means:

We have moved from treating customers as a homogeneous mass to treating each customer as an individual. It means more than understanding the customer as someone with whom there is a transaction—who buys a product. It means thinking of the customer as someone the company wants to "keep for life." The company wants to know who they are, and what their personal relationships, business relationships, and the like are. Understanding who customers are and what their needs are requires maintaining a constant dialogue with them.

This type of marketing strategy applies to every employee and group within the organization, whether or not they have contact with the ultimate customer. A candy manufacturer adopted this individualizing approach with its distributors:

In the last ten years, the pace of customer change was dramatic in terms of customer consolidations within the big channels of distribution that we service. First, there were fewer grocery stores, combined into fewer chains. Then there was the rise of alternative format operations like the warehouse clubs. Before, we had a fairly homogeneous group of customers who bought pretty much the same merchandise with consistent seasonal variations. Now we have a smaller set of individual customers with unique characteristics regarding merchandise selection, delivery volumes, frequency, and price. These changes compelled us to talk to these customers in some depth to really learn what drives their business and what we could do better for them. Now we carry on an ongoing dialogue and look after each other's best interests.

The process of building customer relationships is very similar to the process by which individuals establish close personal relationships. Carl R. Rogers, a noted psychologist, once defined a relationship-building process as part of his client-centered theory of psychotherapy. The following stages are adapted from his theory:

1. Accessibility
2. Accountability
3. Commitment
4. Enhancement
5. Positive regard

The first three stages—accessibility, accountability, and commitment—refer to the formation and maintenance of relationships. When applied to the business world, they suggest that organizations and customers must show each other that they are trustworthy, dependable, and consistent by being open and sincere in their communication. Their communication must be both expressive and unambiguous.

The next stage in a close personal relationship is enhancement, or the desire to grow, learn, and change. In business relationships, this stage means that organizations and customers educate each other about how they can develop within their respective roles.

The last stage is positive regard, which in a personal relationship means love, friendship, and acceptance. In the business world, fifth-stage customer relationships must include expressions of gratitude and acceptance, so that the organization conveys the worth of the customer to itself and vice versa.

This five-stage model echoes the thinking of Harvard Business School marketing professor Theodore Levitt. In his book *The Marketing Imagination,* Levitt suggests that companies previously conceptualized the buyer-seller relationship as a form of dating—plenty of wining, dining, and dancing. And once the sale was made, the relationship frequently ended. Today, he says, customers are more interested in marriage ("customers for life"), and the relationship is only just beginning when the first sale is made. This same approach is equally successful—and necessary—with employees, suppliers, and other business partners.

Let's look at each of the five stages more closely.

Accessibility

One of our research participants used accessibility as the first stage in developing a new niche market. The new market was small business customers, who formerly were pooled in a mass market category.

In the past, these accounts had been serviced by the company's telemarketing department. To increase accessibility, the company assigned account managers to these customers. Account management, they reckoned, would play a major role in customer satisfaction and retention. The account managers were made responsible for managing the customers through regular communication and tracking; for improving customer satisfaction by acting as consultants and problem solvers; for gathering information about customers' needs and about changes in their marketplaces; and for increasing the segment's profitability.

To build this account-management capability, the company had to find out what its small business customers actually wanted. So it held customer expectations workshops. The company invited customers to three-hour working sessions to help it understand what it had to do to make these new relationships work. The sessions were attended by a cross-section of company representatives involved with small business customers, including sales, marketing, distributors, and dealers.

The expectations that the small business customers expressed eventually became the account managers' performance requirements. They included "meeting customer needs" and "having personal relationships." The sessions also established what the customers wanted to discuss with their account managers, their requests for company information, and how they wanted to be contacted.

It took a year for the company to implement this program, but even after the first year, the results were excellent. The company had turned a marginally profitable group of customers into a very profitable niche market.

Once the company had made a commitment to developing long-term customer relationships, it started by opening communication—two-way, frank, and sincere. For a long time companies have used television commercials, newspaper advertisements, newsletters, packaging messages, coupons, outdoor signage, and the like to convey an immense amount of information to their customers. Now companies are moving from such broadcasting to narrowcasting. They want to deliver personalized information to their customers.

One large catalog company uses information about its customers' birthdays to establish closer relations with them and thereby increase business. This company captures information about the name, age, and sex of each child in each customer's household. Then it produces a monthly series of birthday flyers, tailored by age and sex, that offer selections of toys and gifts. The children's parents receive an appropriately targeted flyer with a personalized message, indicating that if they place an order now, they will receive special birthday gifts for their child.

A very important element of accessibility is the ease by which customers can communicate with the company. Toll-free phone numbers or fax numbers listed with products or advertisements encourage customers to ask questions or request information. Since manning telephone lines can be expensive, some organizations are experimenting with voice-mail systems.

> *We have a voice-mail system for our employees—so why not for customers, too? The customers can call in with a question or comment and leave us a message. We get back to them either with a phone call or by allowing them to retrieve an answer from our voice-mail system.*

The future, though, lies in electronic communication. Automakers are experimenting with interactive TV systems that enable viewers to browse among models, watch video brochures, and set up test-drives at the touch of a button. E-mail, electronic bulletin boards, and the Internet are other means of communication. As one company explained, electronic communication sometimes creates bonds with customers that would not normally have developed:

> *For some customers, particularly those halfway around the world, electronic dialogue seems to work best. In fact, I've never spoken to some of the customers who I've been communicating with electronically for years. One of the advantages of electronic communication is that once customers get used to it, they don't hesitate to "call." Surprisingly, screen-to-screen communication enables a very open and trusting dialogue—sometimes even more than face-to-face communication.*

No matter which an organization uses, it must acknowledge each customer communication it receives. This applies equally to complaints, suggestions, and compliments. Ignoring a customer is a quick way to end the relationship.

Every time a customer writes a letter to us, they are called back immediately with a response—usually within twenty-four hours of receipt. This applies to every type of customer, and to every type of communication. We particularly stay in close touch with our frequent customers because we often make changes based on what they tell us. We do relish the compliments. It's nice to be able to thank a customer for their letter or call.

Accountability

Although more communication with customers is taking place electronically, most organizations still strive for face-to-face opportunities to listen and respond to customers. Users group meetings are one formal way that large groups of customers can voice their views. In general, participation in users group meetings seems to increase customer satisfaction—and retention. Customers in such groups get more involved in developing products and procedures, and they know that their suggestions are being taken seriously. This automobile manufacturer found such groups invaluable:

We have an advisory board of two thousand owners of different car model series. The owners participate once or twice a year in a focus group setting to discuss changes they would like to see made in the new models. Smaller groups can also be called together quickly from time to time for reactions to specific changes, such as new service or pricing policies. The board also has the opportunity to attend preview parties for new models. We communicate regularly with the board members, advising them of outcomes based on their input. At one time we offered them key chains as recognition for their participation, but they refused to accept them. They were happy knowing that their input was having an impact.

This medical supply company found that establishing different user groups for each type of user created an even closer bond and even more communicative customers:

We have different user groups based on how customers use our products. There is one for physicians, one for nurses, one even for chief financial officers. These groups educate us on what they need to operate successfully. Before the user groups, only about 30–35 percent of customers responded to our surveys. Now it's 90 percent, because customers realize that the company cares about what they think and that it will respond to their concerns.

Users groups enable communication to large organizations, but true customer relationships are established one-on-one. Even organizations with hundreds or thousands of customers are trying to stay in touch with each customer, usually through some type of calling program. They contact frequent purchasers and long-term customers regularly to find out what they think about the company and its products and services and to surface any complaints—impressions that might otherwise go unspoken. New buyers are also called and asked for the same type of information. One car manufacturer's surveys showed a higher level of satisfaction among buyers who got a follow-up call:

Our dealers are required to place a follow-up call after each car is sold and after each service is performed. The advantages are several. Customers are much more likely to bring up issues during these calls while impressions are fresh in their minds. Our research has shown that there is a much higher level of satisfaction among people that get a follow-up call than among those who don't. Dissatisfied customers can become much more satisfied if their problems are solved in this proactive environment.

Customers also expect that organizations will "remember" what they told them. Relationships are built on history, not on ignorance. Information systems play an important role in maintaining an organization's memory of its customers. The systems can track purchases, service records, call feedback, and personal data for millions of customers. As Figure 7–1 shows, our

Figure 7–1   Most Critical Information Systems Applications

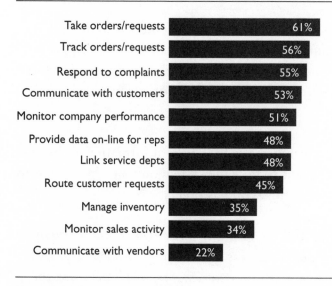

Note: multiple responses possible

research participants consider a company's memory, as well as quick response to customer issues, to be the most critical applications for information systems today.

A top priority for one car manufacturer was to establish a customer database that would help it target its marketing efforts more precisely to *when* customers were looking for new cars.

One of our priorities is to develop a customer information database that will enable us to know where we're at in the ownership cycle with each of our customers. We want to use this information to develop a one-on-one relationship with our customers that we don't have today. For example, if we know that their car is four or five years old, we'll use that information to invite them in to see our new models and perhaps offer a rebate on a new purchase.

This bank also uses its customer information system to provide better service and improve its customer relationships:

Any interaction that occurs with customers is immediately logged into our records. We pay special attention to problems and pet peeves. There's nothing more frustrating for customers than to have to repeat a bothersome issue each time they call.

An airline, recognizing the value of the information in its customer database, plans to take the system onboard its aircraft to create even closer bonds with customers.

We want to be able to wish our passengers a happy birthday and to be able to access information about their travel histories or special meal requirements. We'll also use the system to enter new information about customers. For example, changes in flying patterns can be noted and the marketing department notified to offer the passenger a value package for the new destination.

Commitment

Beyond showing that they are accessible and accountable, organizations need to show customers they are committed to building relationships. Commitment can be represented as the difference between users groups and owners clubs. At a users group meeting, customers see new products and raise concerns. At an owners club meeting, customers interact with company employees. For example, at Harley-Davidson Owners Group (HOG) meetings, members ride motorcycles with local dealers, exchange safe riding tips, and share information about best trips.

One research participant uses community fund-raising events to get involved with its customers:

Our employees and their customers and prospects get involved with each other by buying tables at local fund-raising events and distributing the tickets both to their own representatives and to their customers. A great deal of networking takes place among attendees, with business cards traded across the table. By making introductions for people who can help each other, we position our employees as involved, caring, and trustworthy colleagues rather than as pushy salespeople.

A bank used a volunteer effort to build closer bonds with customers that share similar interests. The event also seemed to increase bank pride among employees and customers alike.

One day a year, on a volunteer basis, bank employees and their families are encouraged to go out and pick up trash strewn on the beaches. The first year, around three hundred volunteers came. Within three years, it was closer to a thousand people. It became such a big event, including media coverage and support from local environmental groups, that our customers asked us if they could join. Now it's not unusual to see some of our best customers out on the beach working shoulder-to-shoulder with bank employees. Now everyone looks forward to the annual event as a family outing and block party. Employees take great pride in being part of a bank engaged in such a worthwhile endeavor. Our customers also tell us they are proud to do business with us.

There is no better way for a company to show that it is committed to its customers than to share a little of the risk with them. This may involve making guarantees for product delivery or quality.

We've gone so far as to have formal working agreements with several of our customers with respect to product quality. These customers actually inspect the quality assurance processes at our factories. Then they agree to let us ship our products directly for use on their assembly lines. In fact, we stamp our products with our customers' quality stamps to show that the products have been tested and verified. Once the products arrive at the customers' door, they go straight into production; the customers don't have to inspect them. We assume the responsibility for product quality and guarantee any lost time in production or lost volume due to mistakes at our end. The result has been

significantly reduced operating costs, both for our cus-
tomers and for us.

Enhancement

Customer relationships grow through mutual learning. For example, a car dealership may offer a free weekend workshop to its customers, describing car operations and simple maintenance techniques such as how to change a tire. The customers learn how to maintain their car and will hopefully reward the dealer when it comes time to purchase their next car. At the same time, the dealer learns what customers do or don't know about automobiles, which can help in future sales and marketing initiatives. For complex products, such as financial services, the learning curve may be much steeper, but it is still surmountable:

In our case, customers need to understand the product, and there is a big learning curve that they have to pass over before they even feel comfortable about investing. The problems begin with taking the first step to become comfortable with financial investments and securities. People have fears about calling. So we provide potential investors with kits and conduct workshops that help people think through strategies for investing by determining risk and reward preferences. Based on their preferences, we can provide them with a basket of different products that serves their needs. Our salespeople approach customers as being at a point on the learning curve, and then as they enter the relationship, the salesperson tries to identify where they are on that ramp of the learning curve. The ultimate objective is to advance customers along the learning curve even-

tually to the point where they are confident, trusting, and profitable investors.

Teaming with customers is an excellent way to promote learning. One company realized the importance of teaming when it discovered that it had lost customers where it had relationships with maybe two or three people at customer sites. Conversely, it retained customers where it had relationships with a dozen or more people. In addition, the company found that the more its employees were in contact with a customer, the more likely that customer's problems were kept small and resolved quickly.

Traditionally, vendors created value in the marketplace through their products. As shown in Figure 7–2, the vendor defined a product's value, which an account representative then sold to the buyer's purchasing department. The interaction took place primarily at the point of sale. Very little contact took place between functional departments, such as between the vendor's logistics department and the buyer's warehousing staff.

Today, vendors create value in partnership with buyers. Moreover, value is as likely to come from people and information as it is from products. In the new value relationship, ven-

Figure 7–2   The Past: Products Delivered Value in Mass Market Selling

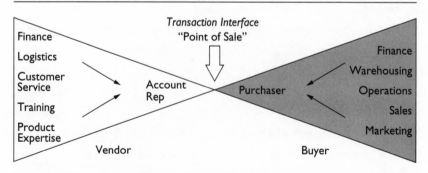

dors act as consultants to buyers. As shown in Figure 7–3, buyers and sellers today interact not just at the point of sale but before and after the sale—at the "points of service." Typically, interaction takes place between teams of employees from different disciplines. For example, the employees at the vendor's customer service department are likely to work closely with the buyer's operations department that uses their product. So complex have the relationships become that the vendor's account representative has become a client relationship manager, responsible for the overall coordination of the different interactions with the buyer. For the buyer, the purchasing department acts in a similar role as liaison.

One of our research participants, a steel manufacturer, found that partnering with customers promotes a deeper understanding of customer concerns and of areas for improvement. Partnering relationships can create a seamless interface between an organization and its customers. As one research participant

Figure 7–3   The Present: People and Corporate Knowledge Create Value in Partnership with Clients

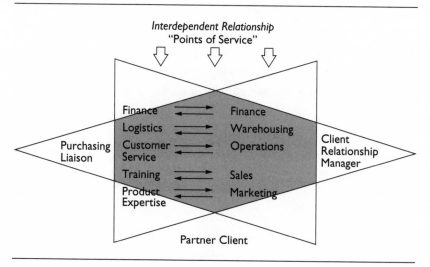

said, "It's almost as if we've extended the manufacturing process right into the customer's shop."

A team of employees is the customer's routine point of contact; it's a direct link to manufacturing. In the past, a customer would talk to a salesman, who would talk to somebody in marketing, who would talk to somebody in manufacturing. Now we solve problems together. Sometimes we actually lead the customers in their own processes. We'll duplicate their processes in house to see where the problems may be. This has also encouraged customers to get us involved earlier in their design process. Now we're designing the parts they need when they're still just lines on paper. We know as early as possible what will work and what won't, and we can make changes without slowing down their production.

Partnerships with customers aren't limited to manufacturers. Service organizations, such as this credit card company, have also realized the benefits of partnering by becoming much more than single-service providers.

We started looking at our corporate customers as more than just users of our charge card or travel service. We've been looking to couple our competencies with their needs. For example, we just launched a purchasing card for corporations to help them with their purchasing systems. For individual customers, we are looking at how we can help be an expense management partner; we want to be more than just their charge card supplier.

The complexity of customer partnerships means that, for any one company, they are generally few in number and are targeted toward higher-value clients who want to create long-term relationships. As such, they require serious attention from senior management. One executive who participated in our research spent a year establishing and working relationships with his company's top customers. These meetings were called "top-to-top" meetings, and they generated amazing loyalty among this very important group of customers. Our research showed that one distinguishing feature of customer-focused companies is that their executives spend significantly more time with customers than do those at other companies, who focus more on financial performance and internal processes.

The benefits of a partnership to the customer are obvious: improved products and services. But the seller also benefits. Our research participants who had partnered with customers said they realized shorter development times and reduced operating costs. One firm reported remarkable savings, reducing its product development cycle from two years to fifteen weeks. Learning brings its own rewards. Companies that become interdependent with their customers are building equity with them. They are differentiating themselves from the competition, making it hard for their customers to walk away and restart the learning process with a new supplier.

How do partnerships work? Like any major initiative, they start with planning. One research participant laid the groundwork with customer-care plans:

Our customer-care plans provide forty hours of free support annually to help customers use our products better. As part of the plans, we also meet with the customers monthly to review issues. The objective is not necessarily to have no issues but to always have new, different issues. We also offer free seminars to educate customers about our products. For those who need more personal attention, we conduct performance evaluations to review how their products are functioning within their operations. The last step in the process is an annual progress summary—which provides an opportunity to discuss prior-year accomplishments realized from the services provided and to plan for the future. The customers prefer working with us on these issues rather than with a third party, because they know we have a vested interest in making everything work for them.

For a partnership to work, it must be based on trust—trust in individuals, products, and processes. It requires a free flow of information, unimpeded by politics or by the desire not to offend.

We call it an open society. That's a partnership. We tell our customers things that we wouldn't normally publicize, and they tell us things. It's a mutually respectful relationship.

The key to successful partnerships is the *desire* to learn and collaborate with customers. One valve manufacturer makes a point of recruiting engineers who don't just want to sit behind a computer and are comfortable being out with customers. It urges the engineers to spend time on the phone, fax ideas back and forth, and visit the customer site to see how its products are used. The learning process is continuous. The engineers, by staying in touch with the customers, find ways continually to upgrade the customer's equipment. They record each new design and improvement in a library so they don't have to start from scratch every time they work on a new project with a customer. In the future, the company plans to give its customers access to its library so the customers can generate a wider range of designs on their own and execute each one faster. They also plan to use interactive audio and video communications to enable engineers and customers to view and discuss designs simultaneously.

Some organizations have found it makes sense to shift the power in the partnership to the customer. They have made it clear to their employees who are part of a team working with a particular customer that the team reports directly to the customer. They feel that only this strategy motivates employees to work on behalf of customers.

The employees, as part of self-directed teams in various areas of the operation, are empowered to function as teams for the customer. These teams don't report to anybody in the company but the customer. Employee reviews are conducted through random telephone surveys of customers by management as well as semiannual customer satisfaction surveys. The teaming arrangement has had a huge impact on employees. They have become much more aggressive not only in raising their education level but in learning about the operations in their own areas as well as throughout the company.

What do the customers say about this teaming?

They love it. They really love it. Why? Because when customers are doing business with your company, they're not really doing business with your company. They're doing business with the people inside your company. That's the relationship that customers really value.

Positive Regard

The last phase of the customer relationship-building process is positive regard. Customers like to feel appreciated by the organizations with whom they do business. Consumer goods companies have a long history of rewarding their customers—offering incentives to establish and maintain mutually beneficial relationships. One automotive company that adopted this approach is considering revising its leasing agreements to reward long-term customers:

> We offer short-term leases, knowing that the customer will be back for a new car in two or three years. In the intervening years, we build the relationship through thank-you letters, special service offers, and birthday greetings. Six months before the lease expires, we invite the customers to the showroom to view new products. We are also experimenting with a long-term/short-term lease that offers the customer a choice of three or six consecutive two-year leases at a fixed monthly payment. This will guarantee a long-term relationship.

All types of organizations are eager to reward their customers for long-term patronage. Frequent purchase programs, which started with airlines, can now be found in retail and service establishments, such as restaurants, bookstores, and hardware stores. Although rewards are often reviled as short-term fads, they can and do build customer loyalty. To be successful, they have to offer things that customers value: cash value, choice, convenience, prestige, and relevance. One airline expanded the concept of reward to include "treating" its Frequent Flyers with special services:

> It's not just the Frequent Flyer bonuses that matter to our customers. Anyone who's flown for eighteen hours knows that personal comfort and recognition are equally important. So we offer upgrades, special check-in procedures, and priority lounges for Frequent Flyers. It's the personal attention and service that keep them coming back.

To be sure, not all customers are created equal when it comes to reward programs. Companies should reward customers who are, or can become, profitable. They need to make sure that the value of the future business that the reward creates is greater than the value of the reward itself. Finally, it's important to stick with the reward program; the benefits are rarely immediate.

The true purpose of a reward program is to change customers' habits so that they become sustainably loyal. The reward offers that companies make will help them identify customers who have the highest potential value and who will increase their patronage. These are the customers that should be encouraged to take advantage of the reward. This credit card company used a reward program to identify zero spenders who, with the right incentives, could be enticed to use their cards:

Zero spenders are customers who have our card and pay the annual fee but rarely or never use it. These customers don't generate much profit and are likely to defect to another card company, so they are an obvious target for a loyalty program. But not all customers in this segment are high value. Some customers are not using the card because they can't afford to; but others are using cash or a competitor's card instead. It's the latter category that we want to target. There's no way we can distinguish the two groups based on behavior, so we have to structure an offer that will encourage the high-value customers to identify themselves. One that worked was an offer of two free airline tickets for heavy card usage in a six-month period. The tickets appealed to the customers we wanted to target—those with high discretionary spending. The cost of the offer was high, but the cost of losing these customers would have been higher. The cost of the offer was still

*lower—and time to market was faster—than it would
have been if we had conducted extensive market research
to identify high-value customers.*

As this example shows, reward programs can be a quick and
cost-efficient way to test many different value propositions and
thereby identify customer segments and desirable buying
behaviors. As we'll see in the next chapter, all this information
can also be used to attract the right new customers.

Such reward programs can be used by all types of companies.
Supermarkets and gas stations have learned to identify high-
value customers through special coupon promotions. In such
businesses, where the majority of transactions are still conducted using cash, the coupons are often structured so as to
gather basic customer information such as name, address, and
type of purchase. This information is then used to build marketing programs targeted to specific customers.

Organizations on the leading edge of customer relationship–
building are venturing into customer recognition *without
reward.* They may, for example, present awards to clients who
provide excellent service to *their* customers. Or they may recognize clients for their service to the community. Recognition is
sometimes more meaningful to customers, they are finding,
than actual rewards—as it is to employees.

*We very much appreciated the award we received from our
supplier recognizing how our services have helped make
our customers more competitive. This was a fitting tribute
to a long and successful relationship with our customers
and our supplier. Frankly, the award meant a lot to us,
partly because we didn't expect it, but also because of the
public tribute.*

IT'S NOT FOR EVERYONE

Developing a long-term relationship should not be the goal of every customer contact. Organizations need to think seriously about which customers they want to get and keep. First and foremost, our research participants caution, select customers who are profitable. This may mean walking gracefully away from customers who aren't profitable—at least not now. Nevertheless, the door should always remain open, just in case these customers become profitable in the future. In the meantime, organizational resources should be shifted from serving unprofitable customers toward developing relationships with profitable customers.

There is one caveat: Customers can be valuable even if they don't generate a direct financial profit. Prestigious customers can be used as references. Other customers can be useful as a first access to a completely new market or act as a beachhead to a big divisionalized company. Still other customers can help suppliers acquire or extend new technological and commercial skills, becoming the partners of the future.

SOUND ADVICE

Retaining good customers means business—increases in revenue and profit. Companies retain customers when they have actively developed the customer relationship. They start by making themselves accessible to their customers. Then they must show that they are accountable, committed, and willing to learn, and that they value their customers. Customer relationships, like personal relationships, don't stand still. They require constant nurturing and attention. Only companies that are willing to invest the time and effort will reap the rewards of building long-term customer relationships.

8

Gaining New Customers

THROUGH RELATIONSHIP-BUILDING PROGRAMS, organizations can develop an extensive knowledge base about customer requirements. They can then use this knowledge to generate new business. Traditionally, new business meant new customers. But since the cost of acquiring a new customer is much higher than the cost of retaining an existing customer, organizations have shifted in favor of increasing business from existing customers.

That said, organizations still need to attract new customers if they are to continue to grow. These customers may be part of a new niche market, or they may be new members of existing markets. What's different today is that when organizations do try to attract new customers, they target selectively. They use information about their existing customers to identify new customers who are most likely to be beneficial—now or in the future. Selective targeting of new customers can dramatically reduce the cost of customer acquisition.

INCREASING SHARE OF WALLET

Companies' primary efforts at acquiring "new" customers usually focus on increasing share of wallet from existing customers. For some companies, this focus starts at the top of the organization but affects everyone:

For every existing relationship, from CEO to small consumer, our CEO is constantly asking: "Are there any other products we can bring to the table? Have they considered everything we have to offer? What else should we be doing?"

Although sometimes overlooked, the first step in increasing business from existing customers is to make sure that everything is being done to *satisfy* them. If not, money coming in the front door may actually be quietly going out the back door. A bank found that this was indeed the case when it looked a little more closely at its business with existing customers:

For years we tracked customer deposit gains. In general, for every $500 million increase in deposits, about $300 million came from existing customers and $200 million came from new customers. We were pleased with our ability to hold on to existing customers as well as to attract new customers. One year we took the analysis a step further. We wanted to know how much more the "satisfied" customers deposited than the "neutral" or "dissatisfied" customers. The results were a shock. The gains coming from the "satisfied" customers ($800 million) and "neutral" customers ($200 million) were almost being obliterated by the losses from the "dissatisfied" customers ($700 million). This was our wake-up call. Now we know that we have to cultivate our existing customers carefully.

Some companies cultivate existing customers through building advisory relationships. In an advisory relationship, the customer expects the advisor to make the buying decision on their behalf, because they feel unable to do so as effectively, and they trust that the advisor will act in their best interests. These relationships are modeled after the relationships clients have with lawyers and accountants. Financial services companies are adopting advisory relationships. They know that often their customers don't want to sort through mountains of financial literature to choose the best products for their needs. Such customers are afraid they'll make the wrong choices. They're looking for help, and they would prefer single-source accountability for all their financial concerns. For the advisor, the end result is more products per customer and a higher share of wallet.

One bank initiates advisory relationships this way:

We start by identifying those customers that have the greatest potential for growth—desirable customers who have a small number of products with the bank. We send these customers a letter inviting them to meet a bank representative to discuss a new approach to dealing with the bank. The letter is followed by a phone call to schedule an interview. At the interview, the bank's advisory approach is discussed. Interested customers are invited to volunteer personal financial information. Then the banker prepares a no-charge financial activities review. The document identifies the combination of bank products and services that best fits the customer's needs, attitudes, and lifestyle preferences. A schedule is attached showing how the plan can be implemented, including transfers of products from competing institutions. Regular interviews are held to monitor customers' changing needs and keep them advised of new products. This approach, we've found, tends to make customers more loyal. They ignore price differentials on products and services and focus instead on the value of the relationship.

One research participant found that its program to retain customers, based on giving free support and advice, was actually very successful in generating new business. The program often identified new areas where the company and its customers could work together. Eventually the new business generated by the program paid the program expenses.

We started a program to offer existing customers forty hours of free support. We considered this to be an investment in keeping our customers. What we didn't realize was that as we started offering support, it opened up opportunities in new business areas. A customer retention program became a very effective cross-sell program. When we first made this investment, we were losing twenty-five customers per year. In five years we cut that number to two. As it turned out, it takes only one or two retained customers to pay for the entire program.

PUTTING DATABASE MARKETING TO WORK

No matter what approach companies use to win more business from existing customers, they are relying increasingly on database marketing. Building large databases and capturing in-depth customer information help companies predict who will purchase what and when, and which customers to target for what type of relationship. One company makes extensive use of its database:

We capture as many as fourteen hundred pieces of information about a household. These include typical demographic items like income and home ownership, appliance ownership, and purchasing histories for various categories of products. Our statisticians have also determined reproducible relationships between individual characteristics and aspects of consumer behavior: who is most likely to respond to a given promotion, to purchase given mer-

*chandise, or to use given credit terms, and at what time
of year.*

A bank uses database marketing to identify prospective customers for new products. First it segments the user base, cate-
gorizing customers as financially secure, suburban climbers,
check cashers, and so on, in a total of ten categories. Once customers have been segmented, demographic and psychographic
information, as well as bank data such as transaction, balance,
and purchase history, are added to the profile. A database
analysis is done to identify which groups of customers are buying what. After a profile has been created, the database is
scanned to identify customers who don't own a particular
product but have characteristics similar to the ones who do.
These are the customers targeted for the new product.

Here's how the bank used the program to promote a check
card that its customers present to make purchases at checkout
counters:

*The database was analyzed to identify current ATM card
users who were considered better customers based on a
six-month history of checking account balances and cred-
itworthiness. The check card was sent to 30 percent of the
active ATM base as a replacement for their ATM card.
Then we developed a calendar for additional mailings to
stimulate use of the check card. Once a month, a different
incentive promotion was mailed to a different group of
customers in an attempt to bring up the activation rate.
Sometimes we offered gifts from merchants where the
check card could be used. The program was a success. The
usage rate was three times higher than when we did blan-
ket mailings to all customers. We continue to market the
card, but next year we'll position the card as a retention*

tool, offering it to our customers who don't yet have their checking accounts with us.

Companies also use database marketing to identify events that indicate that a purchase is about to occur. An address change, a drop in a checking account balance, and an increased credit card balance are good indications that someone has just moved. This may be the time for a bank to offer a line of credit at an especially attractive rate.

In addition to identifying who will most likely respond and the customer's profitability, customer databases can also be used to identify the potential for loss. For example, by studying loan histories, loan companies can find out which customers will switch companies, which will pay off early, and which will go the length of the loan. Based on this information, earnings thresholds can be set. It's not enough to predict who will respond to an offer; companies also need to know whether the respondee will be profitable.

In addition to identifying and enhancing relationships with their most valuable customers, companies are also using database marketing to determine how much effort they must exert to develop and retain *potentially* profitable customers. This process is known as attrition modeling. It not only identifies customers who are about to leave but profiles what those customers are worth to the company. By tracking and measuring past results—understanding where customers are in the life cycle and their responsiveness to past campaigns—and by determining their total potential over time, the company can develop a range of retention actions.

Database marketing in all its forms is circular. It involves developing a test group, rolling out a campaign, studying the response, and redefining the strategy. The process involves learning more and more about customers, and about what makes a successful marketing campaign. The learning never stops, and hopefully the efforts will produce more and more business from profitable customers.

GENERATING REFERRAL BUSINESS

Increasing customer satisfaction can mean additional business from existing customers as well as from new customers. Long-term customers can be a company's best sales force. Some organizations are not shy about using their best customers in just that capacity, and they reward their "sales" efforts:

> *To recruit new car buyers, we invite two to three thousand likely prospects to dinner and a play or concert. The offer is clearly laid out; there's no deception. Come to a complimentary dinner and show, and we'll also display our new luxury car line. There'll be no pressure to buy, but we do want you to see our cars. Rather than relying on the sales force to talk to these prospects, however, we also invite a large number of satisfied current owners to the event. Then we seat the owners and prospects together at the same tables. The owners chosen for the event are upscale positive people, all of whom are extremely pleased with their cars and the service we provide. They are more than capable of providing all the sales appeal needed to win over many of the prospects.*

Many companies, particularly banks, work hard to understand the personal and business relationships of their customers. Such understanding can provide a wealth of new customers. Some companies use reward programs to encourage customers to identify their business associates, friends, and family:

Many of our new customers are relatives or co-workers of existing customers. We run promotions: If an existing customer refers somebody, they get X dollars in their account, and the new customer gets an additional X dollars in their account. We also run promotions for small business concerns to encourage their employees to become retail customers. We set up tables outside their cafeterias for all three shifts promoting our services. People need to understand that there is a benefit to bringing their business to the bank. It's not just prospects here and customers there; there's a direct link.

ATTRACTING NEW CUSTOMERS

Although companies have shifted their emphasis to increasing share of wallet from existing customers, they have not lost sight of the traditional need to attract new customers. One technique that organizations use is to follow up aggressively with callers who request product information. They consider this a service call relative to the prospect's request, rather than a cold call:

We track every individual who asks for information in response to an ad, a mention in a magazine article, a referral, and so on. After we send the information, we follow up to see what more can be done to help the individual. Since the person already has information about our firm, they're much more receptive to the follow-up call. They don't really look at it as a cold call.

Another company uncovered previously unrecognized customer values by surveying individuals who requested product information but didn't become customers:

Last year we reviewed the list of people who requested a product brochure and matched it against our owner database. We conducted a follow-up survey with the people who didn't become owners. We asked them to comment on issues like price, product features, service, and the competition. The results aided our marketing department in reevaluating our product offerings for next year.

Although many companies follow up aggressively on prospects, the "tell, don't sell" approach is still the preferred way to capture new business. This approach seeks to educate customers so that they will *want* to buy a company's product or service. A financial services firm experimented with this type of marketing, with rewarding results:

Instead of giving prospects a sales pitch, we trained a small group of salaried representatives to provide, free of charge, up to two hours of genuine, objective investment counseling. We taught them to accept the customer's final decision without putting up a fight—even if that decision involved investing in a competitor's offering. We believe the customers are in control. We give them the facts they need to make the best decision for their financial futures. This started as an experiment with a small group of representatives. The results showed that these representatives were outselling old-time agents with many times more experience.

While it makes sense for companies to make every effort to win over prospects who call on them, sometimes companies, faced with declining customer populations, have to expand their focus to reach new markets. In the best of all possible cases, a company is the first one to identify and market to a new group. This bank is such a case; it developed a successful approach to market to Generation X:

Generation Xers, ages sixteen to twenty-three, could not feel more different from traditional banks. Banks are stodgy; Generation Xers are hip. Banks are rigid; Generation Xers are flexible. To attract this market segment, we developed accounts where the holders are not charged for any transaction and are not required to maintain a minimum balance—as long as every transaction is conducted at an automated teller machine. Any transaction conducted by a teller that could be handled automatically costs a few dollars. This has been the fastest-growing segment for our bank. We're reaching a younger crowd who are not afraid of machines and value round-the-clock banking. To stay with this group as they age, we'll be offering home banking and adding ATM services.

When it comes to attracting new customers individually, organizations are targeting prospects selectively because of the huge expense involved. This approach requires knowing a lot about potential customers. Especially in new markets, companies may have to rely, in part, on their new customers to help them start operations.

Our industry is deregulating worldwide. Customers, particularly multinational ones, are looking for alternatives to state-owned suppliers. One thing we learned in our home country is that it is vitally important to understand customers before entering new markets. If you don't do this, the risk is that you spend a hell of a lot of money and don't get any good business out of it. Because of the problems and obstacles in new markets, it's even more important to understand the customer so that the customer "pulls you in" and helps you get started.

Many companies identify potential new customers by purchasing prospect information from other companies. Then they develop predictive models through analysis of existing customer databases, with which they identify creditworthy customers who are ready to buy. Specialized catalogs or phone calls may be used to entice the new buyers. Customers who respond to these promotions then become prospects for transition programs, which sort out which of them will be responsive long-term customers and good credit risks. One retailer described its transition program:

We make a series of offerings with progressively more liberal credit terms. Risk is minimized by controlling the terms offered and the value of merchandise until the customer proves to be reliable. Once customers qualify as good risks, we try to maximize their lifetime values. This is done by offering the right merchandise to the right customers at the right time.

In very competitive markets, companies are developing highly targeted marketing programs to acquire the most profitable customers. For example, one long-distance telephone service carrier targeted Frequent Flyers who spend sixty dollars or more a month in credit card calls, plus substantial long-distance calling. To find this group, it purchased Frequent Flyer miles from three airlines covering different geographies—at about one to three cents per mile. It thereby paid a fraction of the thirty-to-seventy-dollar acquisition cost typical of the most desirable customers. The same company has also had great success in purchasing college alumni mailing lists, which produced new customer yields as high as 17 percent. Clearly, broadcast-style mass-marketing efforts, such as newspaper and television ads with low yields (under 0.5 percent), have become too expensive to reach small desirable segments.

Although profitability is a very important factor in seeking potential new customers, it is not the only measure a company considers. At times, just as important is the "cultural fit" between the customer's needs and the company's products and services. This conformity is what builds loyal customers. A computer equipment manufacturer has a system it uses to determine cultural fit:

> We use a scoring system to profile potential customers to see if we want to do business with them. This isn't meant to be arrogant. Our customers are doing the same thing with their suppliers. There are clearly some customers we don't line up with. They may insist on things like having skip lot inspections or dual/triple source relationships that don't fit with the way we do business. We've learned from our mistakes. We've dropped customers because there was no cultural fit. It's tough to let customers go, but the wrong customers can be very disruptive.

A financial services company found that its service approach made it reasonable for them to target both ends of their client spectrum—novice and premium investors—both of whom could benefit from the company's extra assistance:

> We target two customer groups based on their service requirements and value to the company: premium and novice clients. Premium clients have large assets and complicated financial relationships. They can benefit from the

services we provide and our philosophy of single point of contact. Novice clients may not be worth much in the beginning, but our focus on education means that we can teach them how to bring us more and more of their money.

Attracting the right new customers can be just as difficult as retaining existing customers. The good news is that if the latter is done correctly, the former becomes much easier. Learning what's important to customers and how to keep them helps organizations target new customers they'll want to keep for life.

SOUND ADVICE

Winning a new account, while still a thrill for many sales-people, may not be a financial thrill for companies. Unless the new account is targeted precisely, the cost of winning it may outweigh the benefit. Instead, many companies are emphasizing increasing share of wallet from existing customers, a much more profitable way to win new business.

Increasing business from existing customers requires knowing those customers very well. For companies that have thousands or perhaps millions of customers, technology is lending a hand. Database marketing programs can help them identify what new products customers may need and when they will be ready for them. The same techniques can also be used to identify the type of new customer who can be targeted profitably.

While technology is a useful tool, it does not replace good solid marketing efforts. Companies still need to nurture existing customer relationships to increase business and cultivate prospective customers to accept their products and services.

9
Using Technology and Measurement Systems

THROUGHOUT THIS BOOK we have seen how companies use technology and measurement systems to better understand their customers, communicate their customer commitment, develop their employees, provide exemplary service, retain existing customers, and attract new ones. Technology enablers important to customer focus initiatives include customer information systems, database marketing, computer-integrated telephony, and interactive media. Measurement systems include those that address profitability, customer satisfaction, customer retention, and employee satisfaction and retention.

While examples have appeared throughout the book, technology and measurement systems are so critical to the success of any customer focus initiative that they deserve a separate chapter. This chapter focuses specifically on their successful application in a pro-customer company.

TECHNOLOGY THAT SATISFIES CUSTOMERS' NEEDS

One of the first questions we asked our research participants was which of the organization's existing strengths were used to build the customer focus initiative, with an eye toward assessing the contribution made by technology. Their answers are shown in Figure 9–1.

Unsurprisingly, a pro-customer company culture and employees ranked as the top two requirements. But the surprise was that technology ranked third, above things like training programs, client relationships, and company image. The survey respondents, who ranged from top executives to functional managers, realized in retrospect the greater value of technology. Not only could technology speed the flow of business, but voice-mail systems, electronic kiosks, and on-line services could help companies to get to know and provide better service to their customers.

Our further discussions about the role of technology provided another surprise. A few of the research participants found that technology could be used most effectively when it appealed to something beyond customer expectations of responsiveness or reliability. By using technology to appeal to deeply held, basic human needs, such as the needs for security, control, and self-esteem, companies were able to increase customer satisfaction and retention.

Figure 9– 1   Strengths Used to Build Customer Focus

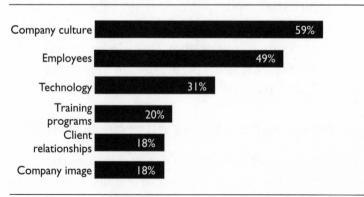

Note: multiple responses possible

Benjamin Schneider and David E. Bowen, in *Winning the Service Game,* explain the importance of satisfying customers' human needs. Consumers are people first, they maintain, and they are driven to satisfy their basic needs for security, esteem, and justice. These needs are more fundamental and compelling than their expectations about service, and often come into play in service delivery. We can all recall service experiences when our expectations were met—that is, the service was provided quickly and competently—but our human needs were not; perhaps we were not treated fairly or with respect. How a company deals with its customers' human needs has a greater and longer-lasting impact on their evaluations of its service performance than whether it actually meets their service expectations.

Technology can be used to satisfy customers' human needs in a variety of ways. Technologies have long been used to safeguard physical security, most recently in home and car alarm systems, 911 dispatch systems, and medical advances. But technology also plays a role in maintaining financial security. The information systems upon which banks, mortgage companies, and brokerage firms rely to process enormous numbers of transactions every day can also watch over an individual's economic well-being. An investment company describes how:

> *We have a computer program that highlights troubled accounts. It flags accounts where balances drop or shift significantly. After reviewing the account activity, management may call the customer to alert them to the situation and provide guidance. For us, technology does much more than process transactions; it helps us maintain our customers' economic security.*

Technology can also be used to satisfy customers' human needs to feel competent and in control, notably in the trend toward self-service. All kinds of organizations—airlines, courts, banks, video stores, and hotels—are using informational kiosks and voice-mail systems to let customers serve themselves. These technologies meet customers' demands for service when they want it (all the time) and where they want it (everywhere). The keys to these technologies are that they have to be easy to use and they have to allow an "out" for people to speak with a human representative. Banks learned this lesson early, when customers initially refused to use automated teller machines because they made them feel stupid.

Control has a strong element of self-esteem. A telephone company gives control to the users of its voice-recognition system, yet allows them a human alternative:

We encourage our customers to use voice-recognition technology. For example, customers can place their own collect calls using it. They can give themselves credit on their bills or order a calling plan for their account. Conversant technology allows them to process their request quickly and completely on their own. A key to satisfying customers with these technologies, though, is giving them the option to leave a system when they want or need to and speak with a customer service representative.

Interactive technologies such as the Internet, other on-line services such as Prodigy or America Online, and interactive telephone services and kiosks may provide some of the best ways for customers to control where and how they receive service, by providing an ever-wider array of functions. The customers of a bank can develop investor profiles using their interactive informational kiosks:

Our customers can create their own investor profiles using the kiosks. They can complete an investor survey that will

help them rank their profile and risk tolerance. The pro-
gram will deliver a recommended investment mix of funds
based on the customer's information. The kiosk will also
produce a printout that can be taken to the bank's invest-
ment officer for further information. Or the customer can
speak to the representative directly through a video link.
The computer may be set up to conduct transactions,
allowing the customer to transfer funds from existing
accounts into the appropriate mutual fund accounts. The
same program that runs on the kiosk can also be loaded
onto a floppy or CD to be given to customers to take home.

Customers are usually able to control service transactions because they have the information to conduct them. At a very basic level, control requires information; people want to know what has happened, what is happening, and what will happen. Self-service technologies make it easy for customers to access information about a company and their accounts with it. Interactive technologies provide an added opportunity for customers and potential customers to learn more about a company through dialogue. Businesses of all sizes are taking advantage of interactive marketing techniques. One small company uses a technique as simple as fax response to interact with customers:

We give customers up-to-the-minute price quotations and
product options using the fax machine. In response, we
receive the telephone number identity of the individual
who requested the information. We can link their number
with transactional data to see whether they're an existing
customer, then mail the appropriate promotional material.

Technology can also play a role in enhancing customers' human need for self-esteem. Companies are more and more collecting information about their customers: demographic, historical, behavioral, and even psychological. They use this information to recognize and reward long-term customers and to give special attention to new customers. Such recognition makes customers feel important and worthwhile. Complex information systems make it possible for companies to collect, analyze, and distribute ever-increasing amounts of customer information.

Unfortunately, customer information is too often maintained on too many different systems, making it hard for companies to quickly access a customer's complete profile. Advances in computer technology, particularly large-scale parallel computers, are eliminating this problem. These machines use multiple high-performance processors to dissect and analyze portions of an inquiry simultaneously, thereby finding an answer much sooner. They can scan massive amounts of data to search for unanticipated buying patterns or clients with particular characteristics. Their storage capacity is so large that they are called data warehouses. So powerful and easy to use has the warehousing software become that companies can use it to launch all types of inquiries about their customers.

Some of the biggest data warehousers are telephone companies. One long-distance carrier sifts through more than four trillion bytes of data to develop *individual* discount calling plans. But smaller companies, like this bank, are also taking advantage of this technology:

*Our data warehouse has details about our customers'
banking activities over the past five years. The database
pulls together information from separate computers that
handle daily checking, savings, and other transactions.
The resulting database yields so much insight into customers' behavior, it's like cheating. Our customer service
representatives tap into it to sell customers all kinds of services while they're on the phone. For example, if a cus-*

tomer is calling to complain about a bounced check, the representative can see how frequently they do this and perhaps offer them overdraft protection.

Technology serves not only customers but employees as well. It can help them become more knowledgeable about the company and its customers, which enables them to deliver information and services more professionally and consistently. Technology, designed well, can also increase employee productivity and thereby prevent customer frustration. Hence it is very important to involve employees in the design of the information systems they will use. Today, information systems are being structured around how service representatives answer customers' questions. As one company said, the purpose of the system is to "keep the facts in the box and the concepts in the (representative's) head."

Technology has to be managed along with an organization's people, purpose, and business processes to project the best service image. Everything must work together; no single element stands alone. Specifically, technology has to be focused on a particular purpose, not just used for technology's own sake. It must be understood in the context of how it helps satisfy a customer's need for security, control, or self-esteem. Organizations that recognize what technology *means* to customers will have the advantage over organizations that recognize only what technology *does* in enabling and delivering service.

CUSTOMER MEASUREMENT SYSTEMS

Our research participants took measurements of every aspect of their customer focus initiatives. Through measurement, they learned whether they had achieved the expected benefits or if changes were needed. They used measurement systems to understand whether customer values are being met and hence whether market share is increasing. First, let's look at a few best practices in developing and using one of the most common measurement systems—the customer satisfaction survey.

It's important to involve all stakeholders in the development of a customer survey. All employees and customers will be impacted by the survey, and they should therefore have a say in its construction. Their up-front agreement must be sought on what is meant by a satisfied customer or an increase in customer retention, on which customers to survey, on which performance attributes to measure, on the timing of the surveys, and on who will act on the survey findings.

Top management commitment is critical to a successful measurement system. If management ignores the measures, so will everyone else. One research participant recommended demonstrating the linkage between customer satisfaction and company profits in order to establish management commitment:

Catchy slogans, even with facts and figures such as "More than 90 percent of unsatisfied customers don't complain," won't necessarily persuade management to commit to customer focus. But if you do a pilot study of customer satisfaction and analyze how much profit can be gained by each percentage of improvement in repeat purchases, management will start to listen.

If top management commitment demonstrates seriousness, then commitment from the rest of the employees ensures that something will happen. Some organizations encourage the various departments to develop more detailed surveys and to review the results in combination with the corporate survey.

Even if departmental surveys are not conducted, it's very important to make the results of the corporate survey meaningful to all levels and locations in the organization.

The measurement system has to work from the lowest level to the highest level. For example, if senior management can tolerate deliveries that are 90 percent on time and 10 percent late, then the 10 percent late has to be understood by division, plant, customer, order, and part number. In the plant, Charlie or Sally needs to know what this means for the parts they handle. The measurements should also be on-line and tied to other systems, such as credit, billing, and shipping. A stand-alone measurement system would fail because of the possibility for contradiction and mistrust. This is very different from the typical one-to-five customer satisfaction rating scale; these measures actually mean something about how people do their jobs.

Involving customers in developing the measurement system helps ensure that it measures what matters most to them. Updating the measurement system regularly with customers can help.

Make sure you and the clients agree on what you are going to do, and then measure against how you do that. A lot of times the customers' expectations can be somewhat different than your expectations, and it takes a long time to figure out what you should be doing or what you think they should be doing. For example, for a long time we thought that product reliability was the key factor in creating satisfied customers, so we spent a lot of time measuring reliability. Then after talking to our customers, we realized that they were less concerned with reliability than with the quality of the relationship with their account executives. They wanted more contact and more information from us. This is what we should have been measuring. If you can sort out the measures up front, I think it helps you implement your service initiative.

Another company uses quarterly business meetings with key accounts to identify what is most important to those customers and measure against those criteria:

Face-to-face business reviews are the foundation of a more formal customer satisfaction program, which we conduct with key accounts at least quarterly. The goal of the program is to move beyond customer satisfaction to what constitutes customer success. We want to help our customers' customers make money. At the quarterly meetings, both companies determine mutually agreed-upon measures of success. Actions taken against these measures are summarized in a quarterly letter, or in some instances monthly. More and more, we are moving toward these company-specific scorecards.

The complexity of customer measurement systems has encouraged some companies to seek help in developing them from consulting firms or other companies. Learning from top organizations can save time and be a real eye-opener.

We picked three Malcolm Baldrige National Quality Award winners to study. We didn't expect to learn much about how they measure success, but we were dramatically mistaken. The visits bordered on religious experiences, and we were converted. We understood just how important measurement can be in driving customer satisfaction efforts.

For Good Measure

Our research participants identified these best practices in measuring customer satisfaction:

- Understand how all business operations can affect customer satisfaction.
- Measure what is important to customers.
- Survey current and former customers.
- Interview constantly.
- Use short surveys.
- Benchmark against the competition's surveys.
- Create surveys that measure cause and effect.
- Measure customer loyalty.

A successful customer focus initiative requires an organization to measure not only customer perceptions but every other aspect of the business as well: people, products, processes, marketing programs, competitors, and financial performance. The reason is that, as we have seen, all these factors influence how customers view a company. The research participants felt strongly about measuring the connection between product and process quality and customer satisfaction. For example, this airline measures every aspect of its customer service processes, in order to understand how they impact customer satisfaction:

We measure every point in service delivery. It might not be something that ultimately touches the customer, but it will impact the level of quality service. For example, high absenteeism at one station will impact on-time performance in a much broader geography. The customers have told us that on-time performance is their number-one priority. If we're late by an hour every single day on every single flight, but we smile a lot, it ain't going to do it. It isn't enough.

A bank tries to tie financial measures to measures of customer satisfaction and retention:

We measure the flow of knowledge from people (new ideas generated and implemented) to structures (new products introduced) to customers (percentage of income from new revenue streams). For example, to gauge whether the structural capital is a support or an impediment, we can measure costs per transaction, improved cycle time, and costs of key processes, among others. Growth in customer capital ought to show up in rising customer satisfaction scores, faster complaint resolution, lowered price sensitivity among customers, and longer-lived, deeper customer relationships.

No matter what aspects of the business are measured, the research participants warned that they have to reflect what is currently important to customers. As one participant said, "When you're still measuring the old things, and it looks like you're doing very, very well, it's hard to tell employees that you're not doing well and you have to change." Some companies also make an effort to get beyond what customers say is important, to what they expect or desire. Again, this analysis must take place constantly: Today's delight becomes tomorrow's expectation.

Understanding the differences between customer needs and customer satisfaction is crucial to hospitals' success. The typical patient satisfaction survey—how do you like our doctors, our nurses, our food—doesn't get at cus-

tomer needs at all. Instead, survey instruments must provide specific information on what customers need in order to chart process improvement plans. For example, after interviewing patients who had undergone bypass surgery, the most common comment was that patients were surprised to wake up on a ventilator. The feeling of panic that patients expressed about the experience was tremendous. They said that no one had ever told them to expect that. So let's suppose that instead of a customer satisfaction survey that asks, "How do you like our doctors?" the survey asks, "How well did we help you understand what it would be like when you woke up after surgery?"

When it comes to customer satisfaction, former customers can tell a company as much as, and sometimes more than, its current customers. Former customers most likely left the company because another company was better at meeting their needs. These people can be a wealth of information about how to improve products, services, or employee performance. One company regularly surveys both current and former customers:

Monthly we survey two hundred customers and four hundred competitors' customers regarding eight "get in the game" buyer values. This helps us determine where we are underperforming and outperforming the competition as part of our strategy to be "better than the best." Then we use benchmarking techniques to focus on improving the underperforming areas.

Measuring the value of lost customers can also help focus attention on customer satisfaction. The dollar value of a lost sale is very easy to understand—sometimes even easier than the value of increased customer satisfaction.

We measure our service quality program using a method called cost of quality. We assign revenue lost dollars to various things and monitor them on a monthly basis. For example, we measure lost business and lost customers. These measures relate ultimately to profitability, and they are easier to use than trying to relate profitability directly to service initiatives.

In addition to lost customers, our research participants recommend surveying:

- a random sample of the customer base
- customers who experienced selected customer service transactions
- customers who complained
- customers whose activity has dropped substantially

Based on these surveys, companies can calculate the return on investment to be achieved from higher levels of customer focus, and they can identify activities that maximize customer satisfaction. Additionally, they can calculate the return on investment from improved complaint handling and determine the attributes that maximize satisfaction and repurchase intention of those who complain.

Customer satisfaction surveys should be conducted frequently because customers' values change frequently. One research participant described their approach as "incessant" surveying:

We survey customers incessantly. We want to know what they expect from us, what they think of the deliverable, and what they think of our attempts to maintain an ongo-

ing relationship. Do they appreciate the follow-up calls, the targeted mailings, the special offers?

As shown in Figure 9–2, a quarter of the research participants conduct surveys continuously. Overall, almost half of the participants survey their customers at least monthly.

One hospital surveys patients continuously using a portable computer:

Our measurement system is a free-standing portable computer capable of reading and analyzing customer needs assessment survey cards. The machine can be wheeled around to different floors in the hospital where patients can answer the survey and insert the responses into the machine. The data can be analyzed by day, floor, day of week, respondent's gender, and the like. In addition to analyzing trends and frequencies of needs, we can get a minute-by-minute analysis of when service is meeting customer needs and when it is not.

Figure 9–2   Frequency of Customer Satisfaction Surveys

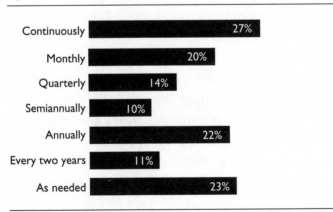

Note: multiple responses possible

Surveys should also be conducted at each stage of the customer relationship. This helps to identify when the customer needs change and whether the organization continues to deliver. One research participant eliminated its annual customer satisfaction survey in favor of the following approach:

- **Expectation studies.** A major undertaking to determine customers' personal requirements and their perceptions of the company (including past experiences) and the competition.

- **Observation studies.** Listening in on customer calls to understand what type of information customers are requesting; the accuracy of the information provided; and customers' suggestions for improvement.

- **Interaction tracking.** A semiannual telephone survey of three thousand customers within twenty-four hours of their contact with the company. The survey compares performance by function and against competitors; evaluates service performance; prioritizes key drivers of satisfaction; and tracks performance over time. The results are compared with the results of the expectation studies to see how initial requirements are being met and what new ones may have been uncovered.

Because time and energy are the currency of the 1990s, shorter surveys can be better than long questionnaires. One hotel chain used to rely on long in-room surveys until it realized that mainly the very happy, the very unhappy, or children were completing the survey. They switched to a fifteen-second questionnaire at checkout. The questions are rotated randomly, but they cover every significant hotel experience factor. The results of the shorter questionnaire were dramatically different from those of the in-room survey. They pointed out what was truly delighting and disappointing customers, and necessary improvements were made.

Customer satisfaction surveys are an ideal opportunity to check out the competition. Companies can find out how their customers rank them against their competitors and why. One company recommends asking customers about best-in-class companies outside the company's industry as well:

As part of the customer satisfaction survey, we ask our customers to grade us versus their best vendors—regardless of industry. Where is our company better than, as good as, or worse than the best. We use a third party to conduct this survey to ensure objective responses. The results may be situational, but overall the information is head-and-shoulders better than a national competitor survey.

Surveys should be constructed to reveal cause-and-effect relationships to identify what company actions may be causing customer satisfaction or dissatisfaction, as well as the relative impact of the various satisfiers and dissatisfiers. This information can help identify actions that will lead to increased satisfaction.

The typical customer survey uses a four- or five-point scale ranging from excellent to poor to measure, for example, the courtesy of customer service representatives. The answers tend to cluster around "good." Unfortunately, this doesn't help you figure out what customer service representatives should be doing to improve perceptions of courtesy. An alternative is to identify the specific behaviors that are linked to courtesy in the customer's view and ask whether each of those behaviors occurred. The overall contact with customer service can then be evaluated on a rating scale. It's much easier to change the frequency of specific experiences than to change evaluative perceptions.

To be a player, an organization must satisfy customers on the basics of its product and service performance. But to build customer relationships, they need to go beyond satisfaction to create customer loyalty. This is more than customer retention. It is an emotional response—recommending a company to a friend, paying a little more for the product, buying again despite recent problems, or returning to the product at the first opportunity. One research participant measures loyalty this way:

We ask customers questions about how our products affect them. Do they feel secure using them? Do the products give them the freedom they want? Their answers to these questions are very different from their answers to questions about their general satisfaction or product attributes. Customers are not so quick to admit that a product affects them. When they do, we delve deeply to understand the reasons why.

Making Sense of Results

A number of our research participants recommend that companies involve employees who interact with customers in the interpretation of survey results. Frontline employees most often know what customers mean by what they say. Moreover, employees need to be aware of the results so they can change their own behavior to better meet customer requirements.

Through the satisfaction survey, a company collects a lot of information from its customers about how it is doing and what can be done better. But you cannot accept that information as representative of exactly what you need to do. You need to share it with the people in your organization who are most knowledgeable and understand exactly what it means and then deal with it. It is not activities, getting people to do things, that brings results. It is getting people to do the right things and the most important things. And quite often we are very eager to do something instead of taking the time to understand what exactly the data are trying to tell us. I would encourage people to spend a lot more time understanding what they have to do and identifying their target very clearly before they commit any people resources to a problem.

One global organization points out how important it is for its local subsidiaries to conduct and analyze their own surveys. Too often, cultural differences between countries or even from region to region affect how survey questions are interpreted or the results analyzed.

We conduct customer satisfaction surveys, primarily by mail, in forty-six countries. We've learned that local management should conduct the research in their own countries because they understand the local market conditions, language, culture, and legislative environment. For example, even a simple 1 (poor) to 5 (excellent) rating scale can cause confusion. Students in Germany are graded in school on a 1 to 5 scale, but 1 is the highest and 5 the lowest score.

Survey results must be examined in the light of other information the company has collected about customers, such as their purchase and service histories. In this way, it can obtain the most complete picture of its customers.

We measure contribution by customer and by product. Are we getting what we like from the customer? Are we selling the products we like to sell them? How many complaints has the customer registered? Are we providing on-time delivery, every time? In addition to the customer satisfaction rating, we also review the feedback reports that customers keep on us. How do customers rate the company?

If done correctly, an analysis of survey results can be used to identify customer priorities, assess existing systems, and determine which areas need the greatest improvement. Our research participants find it helpful to involve the entire organization in the analysis process. Says one:

The survey results are reviewed with every department. It's a two-day exercise, a review product by product and client type by client type. They discuss how the measurement can be improved; how customer satisfaction can be improved; and what behaviors have to be changed. Every department is involved, even accounting. Accounting is the last department you'd think would be involved in service, but the customers were saying the invoices and billing processes were a mess. So accounting did some innovative things, which resulted in accounts receivable days dropping by about twenty-eight. This represented a million dollars a day cash flow. Today, we make sure we ask customers whether they are satisfied with our invoicing and billing procedures.

Customer satisfaction measurements are important company performance indicators. They show where a company is doing well and where it could do better. They can also show the correlation between customer satisfaction and increased sales.

How satisfied do customers have to be before they will buy more products or services? One company used a five-point scale from 5 (high) to 1 (low) to rank satisfaction. The goal was to reach 100 percent 4's (satisfied) and 5's (very satisfied) in two years. But an analysis of the customers who gave this company a 4 or 5 found that actual customer loyalty varied greatly according to whether the customers were very satisfied or satisfied. Customers who gave the company 5's were six times more likely to repurchase its equipment than those giving it 4's. For this company, customer satisfaction took on a whole new meaning.

Some companies are still struggling to quantify the exact correlation between customer satisfaction and increased sales.

> *We calculate how much we're spending on different levels of service, cost per account, and those kinds of items. We know if customers call us and talk to us that they tend to use our product more after that, especially if we were able to help them satisfactorily. But we don't know if we help them with X that their spending goes up by Y, or if we help them with A their spending goes up by B. We haven't been able to quantify it that much. We have been able to establish some linkages, but we haven't been able to say specifically how much.*

Measures of customer retention can also be problematic. This bank tracks the percentage churn in its customer base, but it has yet to calculate which customers it is retaining and by how much:

> *Keeping existing customers and tracking new ones is the name of the game, and the longer the tenure, the more profitability is derived. Our retention remains pretty con-*

sistent. We don't clarify it yet on the basis of dollars or numbers. We track percentage of churn of our business, and the percentages are very low. We are not without defects, and until we have zero defects, we will still have room to improve.

Another way to measure customer retention and loyalty is to survey whether customers select the company as a preferred partner or supplier.

Many of our top customers have identified us as a preferred vendor. We take this title very seriously. The customer is telling us that they want to do business with us before all others. This means we have to make it easy and pleasurable for them to do business with us.

Customer satisfaction and retention are not the final measures. Companies also need to make sure that satisfied and retained customers are profitable.

We've been able to correlate customer satisfaction to increased sales. We also measure retention. And we measure cost of client support. All these measures taken together help us determine whether we're profitable.

After looking at individual satisfaction measurements, companies also examine measures for customer segments. Ratios between segments or between new and lost customers reveal trends. Based on these ratios, companies can see where they are gaining or losing ground and among which type of customers. This helps in developing target marketing and promotion programs.

Finally, companies need to act on what their measurement systems are telling them. They begin by sharing the key findings with all their employees, who must know the results to determine what they should be doing differently. Some of our research participants display the results on tote boards or banners throughout their organizations. Others use on-line dissemination to speed communication. Some hold monthly department meetings to allow employees and management to brainstorm solutions. The sooner employees are made aware of a problem, the sooner they can fix it. Tying compensation to the results is one sure way to create action.

Customers should also be privy to the findings. This helps in the relationship-building process. As one research participant found out, it's not necessary to wait until all the customer problems have been solved:

> I was taking a few of our customers through some of the initiatives we've been doing over the last few years. They were very appreciative and felt it was all great. But they said, "Why didn't you tell us three years ago you were doing this?" We had done it without telling anyone. I said that the last thing they needed was somebody telling them what they were going to do. We had decided to wait until it was finished and come back and tell them that we did it. I got off easy; I think they were right.

As we have seen, the entire measurement process, from design to analysis to action, requires input and support from employees and customers alike. Measurement is a continuous process. Changes made after one measurement cycle are used to improve the next cycle, and so on.

SOUND ADVICE

Technology and measurement systems have both become very important tools in attracting, developing, and retaining customers. Technology helps pull together massive amounts of information about customers and at times actually delivers service. Measurement systems gauge how well a company is doing at each step in the customer retention process, from uncovering customer values to calculating market share gains.

But the utility of technology and measurement systems should not be mistaken for their meaning. The purpose of technology is to help satisfy customers' basic needs for security, control, and self-esteem. Measurement systems are created to guide employees' behavior so that they can understand and satisfy what customers reveal are their ultimate values.

10

Coordinating, Capitalizing, and Continuing

THE PURPOSE OF A CUSTOMER FOCUS INITIATIVE is to shift an organization's focus from its internal financial and operational performance to what matters—the customer. As one of our research participants so wisely reminded us, "We're in business to get and keep customers." Companies grow by attracting, developing, and retaining the right customers. Today, too many organizations have focused exclusively on cost reduction: right-sizing, reducing overhead, reengineering, and rationalizing port-folios. They have realized cost benefits, but often at the expense of growth.

Our research participants agree that the most critical aspect of creating a successful customer focus initiative, after getting started, is coordination. Since the initiative involves everyone in and everything about a company, coordination is necessary to make it a success.

The Unisys Customerize process can help organizations coordinate their customer focus initiatives. It ensures that every aspect of an organization—its people, purpose, processes, and information—is dedicated to serving customers.

One research participant described its coordinated efforts as a pyramid:

On the bottom level, or foundation, is top management leadership and the voice of the customer. At the next level are the motivational requirements, such as customer satisfaction improvement programs and recognition programs. The third level holds "check and decision" processes, which are handled by a cross-functional customer satisfaction committee. All three levels impact the peak of the pyramid, which is corporate culture.

No matter how an organization coordinates the effort, focusing on customers is a big task. It is also very difficult to accomplish; very few organizations manage to undertake all the required elements consistently. Most usually have energy for only one or a few. As one research participant confidently explained, "Our chairman lets any company view what we've done to establish a customer-focused culture, because he knows it's so complicated that no one will be able to duplicate it."

Difficulty, however, should not be an excuse for not trying. Champions of change must be persistent, even annoyingly so, if persistence is what it takes to improve the organization. Start by understanding where you are, what your organizational strengths and weaknesses are, and where you want to go. Then focus on your key goals. Don't try to do too much too soon. Start by working toward goals that are easily obtainable, then build on those successes. This will create the motivation necessary to continue the initiative.

Despite the enormous challenge, 44 percent of our research participants reported that they were highly satisfied with their customer focus initiatives. Only 18 percent were dissatisfied. The remaining 38 percent were somewhat satisfied, feeling that their organizations weren't progressing as quickly as they'd hoped.

But progress can't be rushed. As the research participants emphasized, it is important for organizations to "learn as they go," constantly adjusting their initiatives' goals based on what they discover. Customer focus is not a "one-shot deal"; it is a continuous process.

No organization can avoid focusing on its customers if it expects to survive. Therefore, as one British participant said, "Don't wait till it's too late. The first step is the hardest. Take action and learn—have a go!" Then stick with it—for life. Customer focus is a never-ending process because organizations, even the best ones, are always getting better at building customer relationships that last.

We are the number-one provider of retail and small business banking products, and we have increased our share. But there are at least one or two customers who leave us because they're not happy with us. That drives us crazy.

Index